DELIVERING
POWERFUL
SPEECHES

- **Lose the fear. End the Stage Fright**

- **Capture & convince any audience**

- **Easy techniques to write, rehearse & deliver**

- **Sell products, express ideas, influence your audience**

- **Be a leader, trainer, coach**

- **Earn money as a paid speaker**

Simple charts & checklists for a 1st speech or a seasoned speaker

Carolyn Kerner Stein

Frederick Fell Publishers, Inc.

2131 Hollywood Boulevard, Suite 305
Hollywood, Florida 33020
954-925-5242
e-mail: fellpub@aol.com
Visit our Web site at www.fellpub.com

Library of Congress Cataloging-in-Publication Data

Stein, Carolyn Kerner-
 Delivering Powerful Speeches by CK Stein.
     p. cm.
  ISBN 0-88391-095-0 (trade pbk. : alk. paper)
  1. Self-Help. I. Public Speaking.
  GV995.R55 2004
  796.342--dc22

                                    2005010307

Editor- Jim Barber
Cover and Interior Design- Chris Hetzer, It's About Time Productions
Illustrations- Tim Harrises

ACKNOWLEDGEMENTS

Special thanks and deep appreciation to:

Jim and Grace Barber, *The Barber Shop*, for creative editing, mentoring , friendship and endless encouragement.

Chris Hetzer, *It's About Time Productions*, for designing the book and the terrific cover.

My publisher, Don Lessne, for having faith in my ability.

Roberta Ruggiero, President and founder of the Hypoglycemia Support Foundation.For sharing, caring and always "being there."

Adele Sandberg, for excellent advice, the precise words and for dear friendship.

Donna Horkey, MS, PHR, *The Missing Link*, for always being brilliant and being a fellow Circumnavigator.

Tim Harrises, for artistic talent and creative ideas.

Candance Hoffmann, for guidance, professionalism and good taste

My Gratitude to all those that gave me such kind testimonials.

To the participants in my workshops who taught me to be "Audience Centered."

My associates and role models in The National Speakers Association And Toastmasters International.

To my hero, Jerry Stein, with love

And to the very special people that enrich my life everyday.

Linda Stein, Janet Stein, Clifford Stein
Ariel Fraynd, Daniel Fraynd, Alex Fraynd
Jason Kerner Stein, Kyle Stein

Suzanne Shifman who makes me believe I can do anything!
Judy Stein, Beverly Bedol, Jackie Stein for sharing laughter and tears

PREFACE

Let me confess. I was not always a polished, confident speaker. In fact, there was a time when I actually had to rehearse my name before I could introduce myself.

I'm not kidding. It was many years ago, but I still remember it clearly. I entered a meeting room to attend a networking function. I didn't see one familiar face, so I took a seat toward the back of the room.

A woman at the lectern announced that the meeting would begin with self-introductions. She requested that each of us briefly state our names and professions. As the people in the first row gave their introductions, I listened attentively. After all, this was a good way to know everyone in the room and determine the people who I might want to meet during the break.

Some of the introductions were interesting, some humorous. Several people quickly uttered their names and sat down, other names were hardly audible. Many people remained seated so as not to draw too much attention to themselves. I wondered what I should say and whether I would stumble over my own name.

As my turn to introduce myself approached, I became aware of my heart beating — loudly, it seemed. I no longer listened to the introductions. I was too busy practicing my name! I was actually nervous. Why? There was no reason. Fear doesn't always require a reason. Nonetheless, there it was — STAGE FRIGHT.

What is the secret to confidence when you don't have it? The question in my mind was, "Do I want to be effective, confident, maybe even powerful when I speak in front of a group of people?" YES, without question! Confidence and power feels so much better than fear and self-doubt.

How did I do this? First I began to emulate the people that projected the most energy and enthusiasm. I began to see that fear could be converted to energy, and anxiety could be replaced by enthusiasm. A pounding heart and a tight throat can be recognized as anticipation rather than stage fright.

It took some practice, but I did arrive at the point where I could stand, smile, look around the room and project my name with a clear, controlled voice, with authority and — at times — even with humor.

The basic steps that I formulated became the foundation for my speaking skills workshop. I have presented these workshops around the world to thousands of people. During the years, I have seen dramatic changes and positive results occur with the participants. I've seen people who were plagued with fear, trepidation, and an overwhelming lack of confidence, who — after just a few sessions — could stand and deliver with power and poise.

That is why I know these techniques work. I have put all the best information from my workshops into this book. It is my gift to all those people who have avoided speaking opportunities, to all those people who have felt unable to express their ideas, sell their products, or be effective in front of an audience… in short, to all those people who want to speak, but don't.

The jourrney begins here.

TABLE OF CONTENTS

Preface
Introduction

PART ONE - Break The Barriers   **1**

Lose the fear instead of getting lost in it
Being audience centered
Fear feels real
Fear strikes the famous, you are not alone
Taking the risk
What do you say when you talk to yourself?
Convert fear into energy
Winging it is too much of a risk
A solution for every fear
Quick review

PART TWO - ORGANIZING YOUR SPEECH   **21**

Speeches come in many forms
A keynote address
Seminars/workshops
Sales presentation
Motivational speeches
Breakout sessions
Panel discussions
Being a Moderator
A panelist
Technical presentations
The impromptu
Ceremonial speeches
A Toast
Political speeches
Executive briefings
Facilitating, Training, Coaching, Consulting

The focus and purpose of your speech
Preparing your speech
Topic, event, location, audience,
    Physical setting, format
Sources of information
Organize a simple structure for a
    well crafted speech
The body - the main object
Find your hidden creativity
Using a mind map
Developing your topic
Add spice with humor and stories
The close, the finale, the wrap up
The beginning - grab their attention
A title can tantalize or tease
Use notes that are easy to read
Prepare workbooks and handout materials
How to rehearse your speech
Write your own introduction
Sample introduction
Getting on and off the stage
Quick review

PART 3 - STAGING THE EVENT AND SETTING THE SCENE

The room arrangement
  Chevron
    Auditorium
    U-shape
    Round tables
    Semi circle
    Boardroom
  The projection screen
Doors
Podium
Lectern
Don't put your audience in an oven or a freezer

69

Using a teleprompter
The microphone
  Lavalier
  Stationary
  Wireless
 Lighting the room
Music
Visual aids
  Flip charts
  Overhead projector
  Transparencies
  Fonts
  Electronic whiteboards
  Panaboard
 An event checklist
Quick review

PART 4 - IT'S TIME TO STAND AND DELIVER **93**

You are the message
Watch your posture
Nervous gestures
What shall I do with my hands?
The point is not to point
A call to arms
The "eyes" have it
Things you should never do
Your turn at the lectern
Blushing
Clothes communicate
Take an image inventory
Speaking with style
Defining your style
The Dominant director
The Enthusiastic energizer
The Reliable Responsive
The Analytical analyzer

The style of the audience
Quick review

PART 5 - THE POWER OF YOUR WORDS　　**113**

The pause that refreshes
Your tone, pitch, volume
Monotonous monotones
Practice projecting
Conversational language
Regional Dialects
Common words often mispronounced
Interact with your audience
Involve your audience
Bring your audience into your speech
The apathetic audience
Suggestions for group interaction
Ice breakers
Breakout groups
Answering difficult questions
Keeping cool, credible and in control
Prepare for the pitfalls
Quick review

PART 6 - LEADERSHIP, SELF PROMOTION, EARNING MONEY AS A PAID SPEAKER　　**139**

Qualities of leadership
Conduct a successful meeting
New technology for meetings
Chairing the bored
Meeting checklist
Meeting notice
Meeting action plan
Maintaining control
Dealing with difficult personalities
　　The latecomer

The get up and go
The non-participator
The lime lighter
The broken record
The always negative
The hostile attacker
The side conversationalist
The cell phones
The side tracker
Meet the press
Getting on a talk or news show
Telephone interview
Checklist for a television interview
Clothes and color for video
Earn money as a paid speaker
Marketing yourself as a speaker
How to network
Speaking engagement checklist
Letter of agreement
The traveling speaker
How to speak internationally
Travel arrangement list
Travel checklist
    International
    Third world
    Medical
Personal speaking evaluation
Quick review
Closing remarks
About the speaker

Resources   **189**

Index   **a**

INTRODUCTION

It can happen to you when you least expect it!

You have been asked to prepare a speech and present it in front of an audience. They want to hear your ideas, your opinions, and your experience. Perhaps you have been asked to demonstrate a new product or explain the results of a newly-developed program. Your employer has requested that you address a committee, manage a project, train other employees or prepare an important sales presentation. Your neighbors have requested that you present some issues to the town council. A friend would like you to offer a toast at his wedding.

You are less than thrilled and you don't feel prepared for the challenge. You certainly don't choose to be in the limelight. But refusing to step up to the plate could negatively impact your professional life. Or it could affect your personal growth and keep you from attaining recognition in your industry or in your community.

After reading this book you will no longer need to invent excuses, refuse an opportunity, or dodge a commitment. Together we will travel through the basic steps that will allow you to stand and deliver a presentation to any audience — whether it's an audience of two or two thousand — anytime, anywhere, on any occasion, and do it with poise, personality and power. Not only that, you will enjoy a feeling of confidence, control and credibility.

Here's what you'll discover in *Delivering Powerful Speeches*:

Part One brings you the techniques to break down the inhibiting barriers that have held you back. You will learn how to lose fear and replace it with enthusiasm.

Part Two focuses on the purpose and objectives of your presentation. You will explore how to determine the needs of your audience. You will discover a road map to structuring a well crafted speech and a sure-fire method to tap into your creativity. In short, you'll find all the ingredients that go into the preparation of an informative and expressive speech.

Part Three provides an organized checklist for creating an effective environment for your presentation — all the essentials that make your audience comfortable. This preliminary planning of equipment and logistics is a critical step toward a smooth presentation.

Part Four demonstrates the non-verbal communication that can sabotage a presentation, and the positive body language that creates style and effectiveness for a presenter.

Part Five offers specific steps to verbal power — methods to develop rapport with your audience; a guide to answering tough questions that are targeted against a presenter; and lists of pitfalls (and how to avoid them).

Part Six brings you the marketing skills and leadership qualities that can take you to the highest level of visibility. These abilities will be of enormous help to you, whether you are conducting a meeting, being interviewed by the press, or pursuing a career as a paid speaker.

But that's not all. Easy to follow checklists are included in each part, a self-evaluation list at the end of the book will keep you on track and help you measure your improvement.

Taken together, the six parts of this book are your passport to greater confidence and the highest levels of personal success.

Part 1

BREAK THE BARRIERS

"The mind is a wonderful thing. It starts working the minute you are born, and never stops until you stand up to speak in public."
—Roscoe Drummond

LOSE THE FEAR INSTEAD OF GETTING LOST IN IT

It is comfortable to surround ourselves with barricades. Barricades cushion us, they allow us to stay in a rut, they shield us from taking risks, dealing with change, and avoiding challenges. Barricades hold us back, lock us in, and keep us from the satisfaction of personal development, influence, power, and in many cases — financial and social success.

If you avoid the risk of making a speech or presentation, you will remain just as you are. You will add layer after layer of cement to those barricades. Is that really what you want?

Come along and take a risk with me

Let's break down those barricades and turn them into bridges! Allow yourself to become an effective communicator!

In this book, I will not only show you how to prepare a speech, I will help you develop an effective mind set. When you become more interested in the needs of your audience than in your fears, your fears will subside. Once you are concerned with how your audience relates to your message and benefits from your message, you become AUDIENCE CENTERED —the barricades begin to crumble and confidence envelopes you like a cloak.

FEAR FEELS REAL

Fear is a natural reaction to the unknown. What is fear like? You know the feeling — the symptoms are universal. Your hands shake and your knees tremble. Your throat feels as dry as the Sahara sands. Your heart pounds and your stomach jumps into your chest

.

There could be a hundred fears that hold you back, or there could be just one. Whatever the number, it's important that you deal with your fears. Don't dismiss them. They're not imaginary. They are very real. Those feelings occur when a person thinks about being in front of an audience. Some of these fears include —

Looking foolish.
Going blank.
Losing my notes.
Equipment failure — at the worst possible time.
The audience knows more than I do.
They will ask questions I can't answer.
My hands will tremble.
My voice will crack, or no voice will come out.
I hate being the center of attention.
I prepared the wrong material.
The audience is bored and they do not like me.
I look fat, thin, old, or too young.
I don't know what to wear.
I won't be perfect.
I will freeze.
I will throw up!

Believe it or not, all of these feelings can be channeled and even reversed. You can replace those terrors with positive feelings of energy and enthusiasm.

Fear goes beyond mere physical symptoms. When fear controls you, it limits you from accepting new opportunities. It distracts you by allowing your assessment of yourself to be unjustly harsh. This becomes a strain and puts you into a mindset of negative apprehension. It zaps your energy.

Succumbing to fear is like taking a trip on a rocking chair. It gives you something to do, something to think about — but you certainly don't get anywhere.

Dr. Gary Zukov, author of *"The Seat of the Soul*, states, *"Fear distracts you from whatever you want to do. It clouds clear thinking and perception. It impedes judgement. There is no power in fear. If you choose fear, you choose pain."*

It may seem hard to believe that you can master your fears, but it's true. It is simply a matter of following a set of techniques that require risk taking, learning the language of positive self-talk, and following some easy steps to organize your speech. You may doubt what I'm saying, but how can you know until you have tried it?

The goal is to control your fear, instead of letting fear control you.

How can you do that? First of all, don't think of your speech or presentation as a performance where you must be perfect. The battle with the beast of perfection may not be worth the time or effort. The great fear of not being perfect, that you will look foolish, become embarrassed, and be judged harshly by everyone, is not true..

Here's an example; Canadian singer Caroline Marcil was invited to sing "The Star Spangled Banner" at a Canada-USA hockey game in April 2005. She began to sing, then forgot the lyrics, began again, and as the audience booed, she became flustered and forgot the words again! To make matters worse, as she turned to retrieve the sheet music, she slipped and tumbled onto the ice. She felt her career had ended.

If she had let her fears control her, she would have never have performed in public again. Instead, she appeared a few days later on ABC's "Good Morning America" where she sang the American National Anthem without a flaw. She received a double amount of good publicity to boot!

You can make mistakes, and people will forgive you. You can stumble, and yet you can learn from each speaking blunder. Remember perfection is *not* the goal of your presentation. Instead, you should consider each speech as an opportunity to convey information and benefits to your audience.

Dale Carnegie said, *"We can overcome our fear by action. We generate fear by sitting still."*

FEAR STRIKES THE FAMOUS, YOU ARE NOT ALONE

Stage fright affects many well-known celebrities. Barbra Streisand once appeared on a popular talk show and confided that she has always been tormented with the fear that she will forget the words to her own songs! She feels a deep commitment to her audience and never wants to disappoint them, so she will only perform if there is a teleprompter.

I saw her at one of her last live appearances in Las Vegas for the New Year's Eve Millennium Show. She said that evening that presenting in front of an audience was too great of a strain and she would never do it again. Although she looked great and sounded wonderful, she let her fears hold her back.

There are others. William Hurt, the actor, felt paralyzed by stage fright until he learned that good posture helped "unblock his energy." Try it yourself — shoulders back, head high. Feel the energy!

Donny Osmond refers to his stage fright as a "social anxiety disorder." Although he has appeared before audiences for years, he was overcome with fear when he had the lead on Broadway in *Joseph and His Amazing Technicolor Dream Coat*. Why? He was filled with anxiety because in 1982 he was in the Broadway musical *Little Johnny Jones* that opened and closed on the same evening.

He said that the terror in his heart almost stopped him from accepting the role of Joseph in the Andrew Lloyd Webber musical. He finally overcame his anxiety when he understood that his fear was of failing, and that it was OK if he was "less than perfect." He took the risk and accepted the part. He received rave reviews for his performance.

Dr. Norman Vincent Peale said that he was terrified of speaking to groups during his college years. But because he had a great message in his heart that he was anxious to share with the world, he practiced public speaking until he overcame his fears. He became a renowned speaker for 70 years.

You may not have a great message to impart. You may not choose to become a renowned speaker. BUT, you can be called upon to share your ideas, sell your product or influence an audience. You might as well take the steps to be effective. After you follow the techniques that are in this book you could surprise yourself and become POWERFUL!

I have been hired by the Republican National Committee to be a media image advisor at six of their national conventions over the past 20 years. And just to be impartial, I was hired by the Democratic National Committee when their convention was in New York. It was a great opportunity to observe many prominent speakers just before they walked to the podium to address millions of people on live television. There I was with a roomful of legends, The Reagan's, the Bush's, Billy Graham, Tom Selleck, the Dole's, the list goes on and on.

I was armed with a lint brush, hair spray, Kleenex and Visine. I remember how Betty Ford, Barbara Bush, and Laura Bush were totally relaxed. They engaged in conversation, tea, and photo opportunities before their appearances.

Helen Hayes, the first lady of the American stage, was one of the presenters and I had the opportunity to talk with her. I was amazed when she told me she has always battled stage fright. She said, "When I was in films, we did many takes until the scene was perfect. In the theater, we rehearsed until the words were our own, But a live guest appearance on television? That is very unnerving!"

She told me her technique to overcome anxiety. She would check her posture, smile and remind herself of the words of Helen Keller — *"Life is an
adventure!"* And with that, she entered the stage to face her audience.
"Oh, and don't forget to breathe," she added.

TAKING THE RISK

Why take a risk? After all, if you never take risks, you will never experience change and growth. Everything in life involves some type of risk. You took a big risk when you learned to swim, to ride a bicycle, or to drive a car.

After all, you could drown, fall or crash!

Another risk you can take is allowing yourself to be vulnerable when you stand up and speak to an audience. It's no wonder that people fear speaking in public!

However you should not take *every* risk — just the risks that reward you in some way. To determine whether a risk is worth taking, ask yourself these three questions:

1) Will I regret not trying?

2) Win or lose, succeed or fail — will I be proud of myself for trying?

3) What is the worse thing that can happen if I try? (Keeping in mind that I could have a lot to gain!)

What's the worst thing that can happen? Let me describe my "worst" experience.

A few years ago I was asked to be the guest speaker at the North Miami Mayors Economic Task Force breakfast. I was totally prepared, I was filled with enthusiasm. I was dressed impeccably in a very professional gray pin-striped suit. My make-up was perfect. I was having a good hair day. What could go wrong?

The meeting began, and I was introduced. I stood up, took the microphone in my hand — and just at that moment, I felt something soft around my ankles. I looked down... and there was my skirt circled around my shoes. I never even felt the button pop!

Was I embarrassed? Of course I was… almost as embarrassed as the audience. But I stood my ground, and with one hand held the microphone and with my other hand picked up my skirt. And I began my speech by telling the audience the words I remember my mother (and probably your mother) used to say — "Always wear clean underwear." Well, talk about giving your audience more than they expect!

I lived through it! Now I think you'll agree, nothing could get much worse than that. But not only did I survive the experience, it gave me great material for my keynotes. In fact, it has become one of my "signature" stories and always gets a great laugh from my audiences.

Learning to be an effective speaker is very much like learning to swim. You can read and study, but it really comes down to just "doing." When you're learning to swim, words cannot adequately describe the sensation of the current against your body when you first enter the water, or the experience of floating when you lift your feet off the bottom. First attempts at swimming feel awkward. Fear and trepidation accompany your every move — especially when a big wave hits your face. With a little patience and practice, all these sensations become second nature, and there you are — swimming!

In the same way, words cannot describe the sensation of standing in front of an audience that is reacting to your words. All those eyes filled with expectation staring at you. As you begin to feel your control of the room, you start to experience the power of the platform. It is then that you relax, and begin to feel spontaneous and able to respond to your audience.

I still remember the very first time I made a humorous off-the-cuff remark that I did not rehearse. To my surprise, the audience laughed! That is when speaking became fun for me.

How can you "dip your toes" into public speaking and take a small risk? In my workshops I have each of my participants prepare a five-minute speech, which they then present to someone else in the group. Then they present it to a group of three, then six or eight, and finally to the entire group. After each presentation we discuss the experience and assess the feelings of anxiety that each person felt, along with the strengths and areas that need improvement such as voice and body language.

But if you can't attend one of my workshops, one immediate step that you *can* take is to join Toastmasters International, a non-profit organization with clubs throughout the United States, and even around the world. Toastmasters clubs conduct regular meetings (at least monthly, and often weekly), and each clubs' goal is the same — to promote good communication skills. Most clubs are composed of a small group of friendly and very supportive people. Toastmasters is an excellent source of public speaking training.

Now that I survived my skirt-falling incident, have my speaking experiences been problem-free? Hardly, I have survived hostile audiences, I have survived tired and disinterested audiences. I have tangled with tangled microphone wires; I have used microphones that squealed like an air raid siren while it died in the middle of my words. I have tried to talk over waiters that refused to stop clearing and clanging dishes. I have even talked over waiters who asked my audience if they wanted decaf or regular coffee — in voices louder than mine. I have been in overheated meeting rooms that felt like ovens, while others bore a chilling resemblance to the Arctic Circle. I have lost my notes, gone "blank" with my notes in front of me, forgotten my speech, left my notes in the car, run out of material, and run out of time.

I certainly didn't enjoy those experiences... but I did learn that things happen and they can be dealt with. Best of all, I learned that many times pitfalls can be prevented.

WHAT DO YOU SAY WHEN YOU TALK TO YOUR-SELF?

Many years ago I had the unique opportunity to attend a "self talk" training seminar in Phoenix, Arizona, taught by Dr. Shad Helmstetter, author of *What Do You Say When You Talk To Yourself?* It was there that I learned the importance of positive "self talk" and how it relates to our thinking, our feeling, and our belief system. It was a turning point for me because I had spent most of my life believing what I told myself — and it wasn't all that positive.

You know, we really do talk to ourselves all the time. Sure it's called thinking, but sometimes that voice is so loud it takes over our mind and body. Without realizing it, we often make negative suggestions to ourselves — and our subconscious mind believes everything it is told.

True or not, it accepts what we tell it, feeds and amplifies the same thoughts back to us. Words like "I'm afraid...," "I can never...," "I would never...," "I know that I will fail...," "nothing works for me...," "it's going to be a really bad day" and "I am just not lucky" program our thinking, and we believe what we tell ourselves. Is it any surprise that negative thoughts consume more energy — and cause more problems — than positive self-talk?

I have found that when negative self-talk is replaced with positive self-talk. It fuels our energy, and our fear dissipates, dissolves and disappears.

Try it! All you have to do is say these words..

I feel energetic!
I am excited to be here!
I have prepared and rehearsed and I am focused!
I know my topic!
I am centered on the audience and their needs!
I have information that will benefit my audience!
I am enthused!

You will find that if you say the words, the attitude will follow. This is called "fake it 'til you make it!"

Furthermore, if your self-talk is concerned with the needs of your audience and what you have to offer them, your body will be filled with positive energy. Placing the needs of your audience in front of your own fears allows you to become "AUDIENCE CENTERED" and what a difference that makes. Your confidence level will rise and you will proceed with power.

Are you concerned about your pounding heart or your racing pulse? Don't be! You want to feel that adrenaline rush. It makes you alert and energetic, and puts color in your face. It puts extra horsepower at your disposal. All kinds of chemicals kick in and your mind sharpens. All of these things harness your fears, and YOU HAVE NOW CONVERTED FEAR INTO ENERGY!

It's unusual for someone to succeed on their first attempt, or even a few attempts. You may not get a standing ovation either. Just as your success with public speaking is not built on a single speech, neither is your credibility destroyed if your first few speeches are less than successful.

The important point to remember is that your audience doesn't expect perfection. Most of them would never stand up and be a presenter. The audience just wants information they can use. Information that effects them and is directed to them. Give them a main point with facts to back it up. Bring it to them with enthusiasm and eye contact. They want to walk away and feel that they "got" something. Most of all they want to know you care.

Realize that it doesn't require an audience or a stage for you to practice your speaking skills. You speak to other people every day of your life, and you are usually trying to convey some information or get your point across. That's speaking!

How well your information and ideas are accepted is a measure of your speaking skills.

"Whatever you tell yourself, you believe, what you believe, you become"

WINGING IT IS TOO MUCH OF A RISK

When you need to make a presentation, a great way to boost your confidence is to take the time to organize your thoughts, research your material, and rehearse. You can take much of the terror out of presentations by setting aside time to organize and structure your ideas, to focus on identifying your audience and their needs. With the use of a few checklists (which you'll examine in Part 2), you can properly set the stage, arrange your notes, check the audiovisuals, and in general feel prepared. These steps will significantly reduce any anxiety you may feel.

Some people suffer from a bad case of "never-enough-time-to-prepare" syndrome. It can be challenging to determine the right amount of time that you need to prepare and rehearse your presentation. But if you follow the checklists in parts two, three, four and five, you will be much more on-track with your preparations.

Many speakers say that once they get a few moments into their presentations, the fear vanishes. For them, it is the hours (or days) *prior* to the speech that causes them the most anxiety, and not the speech itself.

The best remedy for pre-speech jitters is to prepare in advance — arrive early, check the room and your supplies, review your notes and greet your audience. Becoming acclimated to the room, seeing where you will be standing, where your audience will be, and picturing in your mind how you will approach the podium — all these things will make you feel prepared. By being prepared, you will be using the magic formula that experienced professional speakers depend upon. "I AM FULLY PREPARED"

The following list is a solution for each of the most common elements of stage fright.

REPLACE FEAR WITH A SOLUTION

Dry mouth
Drink tepid water (cold drinks constrict the throat). Don't drink milk products or caffeine

Shaky weak voice
Project from your diaphragm; bring the sound from the upper part of your stomach. Raise the volume of your voice to reach the back of the room.

Sweating
Apply an antiperspirant to your hairline prior to the presentation.
Dust some translucent powder on your hairline. Carry a handkerchief

Hands tremble
Place notes on the lectern. Use broad expansive gestures. Don't keep your arms rigid and tight to your body.

Jell-O legs and wobbly knees
Take a few steps Do *not* lock your knees. Plant your feet firmly on the floor about 12 inches apart.

Pounding heart
Take slow deep breaths. Remember that no one else can hear it. Think of it as your boundless energy and enthusiasm.

Going blank
Have your notes in outline form at the podium. Use a large font for easy reading. If it happens, say to your audience "Now let me review" — this gives you time to recover.

Losing your notes
Always carry two sets of notes. Rehearse until you know your outline and key points without using notes.

REPLACE FEAR WITH A SOLUTION

Equipment failure

Plan alternatives in advance. Do not be totally dependent on mechanical tools. Prepare handouts with your PowerPoint slides printed on them

Looking nervous

Remember that your fear doesn't show, especially when you look at a friendly face in the audience and smile.

There may be questions that I cannot answer

Prepare in advance for probable questions, and hostile questions (see Part 5).

Other things that you can do to ensure the success of your presentation include:

Determine the needs of your audience beforehand.
Schedule adequate preparation and rehearsal time.
Arrive at the meeting room early to become comfortable with the room arrangement and the equipment, and to meet your audience.
Repeat your positive self-talk to yourself — and believe it!
Remember to breathe. When you are tense and apprehensive, you tend to take short breaths, which rob you of oxygen. Put your hand on your diaphragm and breathe deeply and slowly. Breathe in through your nose and slowly expel the air through your mouth before you begin to speak. Your breathing will become relaxed and normal. This will give power to your voice and oxygen to your brain.

QUICK REVIEW

FEAR ZAPS YOUR ENERGY

THERE IS NO POWER IN FEAR

WE CAN OVERCOME OUR FEAR WITH ACTION

SET YOUR MIND TO BE "AUDIENCE CENTERED"

CHANNEL FEAR INTO ENTHUSIASM & ENERGY

POSITIVE SELF TALK FUELS ENERGY

TAKE A RISK, LIFE IS AN ADVENTURE

ORGANIZE AND PREPARE IN ADVANCE

ARRIVE EARLY

JOIN TOASTMASTERS

Part 2

ORGANIZING YOUR SPEECH

"When I am preparing a speech, I spend two-thirds of the time thinking about what they want to hear, and one-third about what I want to say."
— Abraham Lincoln

ORGANIZING YOUR SPEECH

SPEECHES COME IN MANY FORMS

We have many opportunities to be called upon to speak to a group of people. On all of these occasions, would it be to your benefit — and the benefit of your audience — to be organized, convincing, captivating, and influencing? This portion of the book focuses on how to organize your presentation to achieve those qualities.

First let's define the different situations that call for an effective speaker. The size of your audience doesn't matter — a speech can be presented to an audience of two or *two thousand* people. It is a vehicle to enlighten, entertain, inform, inspire, motivate and persuade. It can challenge people to action, or bring people of diverse interests to common ground. It can be formal or informal. It can last a few minutes or an entire week.

There are some common elements to all speeches, and we'll consider them shortly. First, let's consider some different forms of speeches:

Keynote Address

This is the major speech at a meeting and can be either the kickoff or closing speech. The purpose of the keynote is to tie together all of the components of the meeting. It often offers a strong, passionate and motivating message that sets the tone and theme of a conference or meeting, as well as its priorities. It should contain facts that relate to the conference. A good keynote will offer substance, address the issues at hand, inspire the audience and offer them positive direction. A keynote must have a strong structure, contain many word pictures, be packed with factual and current information, and finish with a strong closing.

Seminar or Workshop

A seminar or workshop is a meeting that provides for an exchange of ideas. It is organized around a strong pre-planned agenda and has an interactive hands-on approach. It can be as short as an hour, or it can span an entire month. A skilled facilitator will vary the delivery of the material to appeal to the different learning styles of those attending. (See Part 5)

When you are planning a seminar or workshop, you should gather as much information as possible about the participants beforehand. This enables you to customize the meeting to that specific industry and that particular audience's needs. This is most effectively done by a questionnaire or an interview prior to the workshop.

A workshop is usually more of a hands-on meeting than a keynote. Audience participation is normal, and physical activities are generally involved. Both seminars and workshops usually utilize workbooks or manuals.

An excellent method of beginning a workshop is to have the participants break the ice by introducing themselves. Self-introductions warm up the room. I also provide name "tents" to place in front of each person so that I may address them by name. I can't depend on my memory.

I strongly advise that in any workshop you let the audience know the agenda of the meeting from the very start. I often begin by asking every member of the group, if the audience isn't too large, what they expect to gain from the time they spend in the workshop. I then write those topics on a flipchart. (Yes, I still use an old-fashioned flipchart, on occasion). I save the sheet and review it at the end of the workshop so that I can make sure that we covered the material that was important to them.

In my workshops I usually introduce role-playing, small breakout groups, and activities that promote an interactive exchange of information.

Sales Presentation

A sales presentation is structured to show the needs and benefits of the product or service that you are promoting. You are presenting a solution to the problems, needs, or economics of your audience.

Selling involves being informative, supporting claims, anticipating objections, showing benefits, being flexible to accommodate questions and interruptions (such as cell phones) throughout the presentation. You need to appreciate the time constraints of your clients. It's important to use visuals — but don't be dependant on them (in case something goes wrong). Most of all, understand that a good closing technique is vital.

A good formula to follow is:

- Know your product.
- Research your customers' requirements.
- Understand their current situation.
- Propose a solution.
- Explain the benefits.
- Listen to the customers' objectives.
- Answer all of their questions.
- Propose the implementation of your solution.
- Ask for a commitment.
- Follow-up afterwards.

Although you should be thoroughly prepared, never go on autopilot and sound "canned." Involve the prospect in your presentation; this creates a feeling of ownership while focusing on value and benefits. Most of all, a good sales presentation involves being a good listener. When you are doing all the telling, you are not really selling.

Motivational Speeches

Motivational speeches tend to be uplifting and entertaining, yet they should also convey a message. Today, most organizations are seeking solutions to business needs. They are looking for content as well as motivation. Consequently, many organizations are using in-house speakers with extensive knowledge of their industry.

Unfortunately, motivational speakers are perceived by some as long on enthusiasm but short on content. Their presentations are often accompanied by theme music from *Top Gun* or *Chariots of Fire*. The audience cheers wildly as they are led to the top of the mountain. However, within a few hours they are back where they started, they return to their offices to find that nothing has changed. It was just a shot of feel-good Valium that quickly wears off.

Motivation will always be an important ingredient in any presentation. Today's CEOs want speakers who not only inspire, but bring useful information that attendees can take back to the workplace. Meeting planners have become sophisticated and they no longer want empty "rah rah" rhetoric filled with change-your-life platitudes.

Speakers, who are authors, or have achieved success in business, overcome a challenge or tragedy and are able to present real tangible substantive material — will always be in demand as speakers. Tony Robbins and Zig Ziglar are excellent examples of great motivators with substance.

Breakout Session

This type of session is a "meeting within a meeting" and it is often held concurrently with other such sessions. A large general session starts the day, and then the audience breaks into smaller groups.
The small groups can provide a good environment for discussing issues and targeting specific information.

Breakout sessions are conducive to forming focus groups and they allow more inter-action of the participants. At times, small groups can achieve what large groups cannot. A small session certainly allows more opportunity for the audience to express their ideas and ask questions. Using round tables helps bring the group together and allows for more individual participation.

Panel Discussions

A panel discussion is composed of a group of three to six people, led by a moderator. The varied composition of the panel can reflect different — and often conflicting — views. This is an excellent way of bringing several viewpoints to the audience, and allowing audience members to ask questions, directed either to an individual panelist or to the entire panel.

Moderator

A moderator should be in touch with the panelists beforehand to give them the guidelines of the discussion, the time constraints that they'll be operating under, and the topics that they can expect. This will help them be prepared to handle challenging questions.

At the start of the session, the moderator has the responsibility of introducing the panelists. In addition, the moderator fields the questions that are asked by the audience,repeats the question and, directs it to the suitable panelist. Quite often, more than one panelist may respond to the same question. Which can bring in another point of view.

The moderator should be prepared with an opening and closing statement as well as questions for the panel in case the audience is reluctant to start the questioning. The moderator is responsible for controlling the time available for each panelist to answer questions. At the end of the session, the moderator should offer a summation and thank the panelists for their participation.

Panelist

Every panelist should know how much time is allowed to present his or her views, how many other panelists will be presenting, the focus of the topics to be discussed, who the moderator will be, and whether a summation will be allowed. The panelist should come prepared with a bio or introduction for the moderator, and prepared information to present to the audience. While sitting in front of the audience the panelist should utilize good posture, remain alert, avoid looking bored, and listen respectfully to the views of the other panelists without interrupting.

Presenting Technical Material

Technical information is the detailed material of a business, financial or scientific nature. In our ever-changing world, it has been estimated that technical knowledge doubles every two years, and this wealth of new information must be conveyed to employees and customers constantly.

A technical presenter needs to be aware of the level of expertise of the audience and how informed they are on the topic. In other words, you must walk a fine line between overestimating or underestimating the knowledge-level of the audience.

An effective method to gauge the expertise and expectations of the audience (if the audience is not too large) is to involve them in the program, right from the "get go." Throw out questions to the audience, or invite questions. Another effective technique (if the group is relatively small and they don't know each other) is to begin with self introductions.

Printed reference material such as handouts or workbooks should reinforce the information that is being discussed. The presenter should concentrate not only on what the participants need to know, but also how much they can absorb. If an audience is fed too much information at one time, the information can turn into a mental blur.

Start by presenting the concept that you want to convey, and then follow with analogies that will help them form a mental picture. Use illustrations, visual aids and examples to drive the information home. Although it can be helpful, don't depend on PowerPoint, cute graphics or overhead slides to convey all the information. Simplify statistics, and make sure that graphs and charts are colorful and easy to read.

Be sure to allow time for questions. Whenever possible, demonstrate what you're talking about. Remember that you can easily exhaust an audience with an overload of data, details, demographics and decimal points.

Of course, you need to be interesting as well as informative. It's a challenge for anyone to stay focused when the presenter is spewing out data in a dull monotone. On the other hand, technical audiences are usually skeptical of too much style and enthusiasm. They are looking for focus on the content and details. Be professional, don't be flashy.

Use effective gestures, maintain eye contact, utilize vocal variety, move away from the lectern and toward your audience. These are the techniques that can make a technical (or any) presentation more appealing. And YES, humor *is* appropriate in a technical presentation.

Here are tips for conducting an effective technical presentation:

- Organize your material.
- Use the correct terminology.
- Define all unfamiliar terms.
- Don't just jump into the technical material; instead, first give the audience a reason to listen.
- Technical presentations are information-dense, so don't let the main message get buried in an avalanche of detail.
- Condense the information to bullet points.
- Make your visuals big and bold, easily seen.
- Prepare handout sheets with your PowerPoint slides printed on them.
- Use only one idea on each slide.
- Don't turn your back to the audience to read your slides.

- Check if you need to clarify what you've said before you advance to the next point.
- Don't kill your audience with information overload.
- Introduce one idea at a time.
- Use a strong summation closing that wraps up the entire session.

<u>The Impromptu Speech</u>

Have you ever been called upon to say just a few words to a group of people on the spot, without any preparation, notes or rehearsal?
Oops! I am caught now and panic has set in. That is called an impromptu speech. The best part about an impromptu speech is that you don't have to spend much time worrying! A good way to learn how to speak-off the cuff is to join Toastmasters International (see Resource Page) where you will learn how to "think on your feet!"

If you are asked to speak and you have no time to prepare, don't panic. Just follow these five steps after you take a deep breath.

1) Think of one main point that you want to convey.
2) Begin by asking the audience a question that relates to your main point.
3) Present that main point.
4) Add a story, illustration or example to bring home your point.
5) Conclude with a summation.

Believe it or not, you can actually practice impromptu speaking. One effective method is to pick a subject (anything from insignificant trivia to important issues), give yourself 30 seconds to plan those five steps just described, and then speak for two minutes.

Another exercise is to walk around your home or office, pick up any object and begin to describe it. Relate to yourself how you feel about the object, what is its function and how it relates to other things in the world. It may sound silly, but if you do this five or six times you will notice that you are able to think on your feet faster than ever before.
Impromptu speaking is a valuable social skill. Picture yourself in these situations;

Scenario 1

You have just been informed that a meeting will be held in fifteen minutes, and you will be expected to present your ideas and opinions.

Scenario 2

At the very last minute, you are requested to say a few kind words about…..

Scenario 3

An event has just taken place, and you are a witness. "Please express your feelings."

The five steps given above, are effective when you are asked to "say a few words" without prior notice. What about an entire speech? Is it possible to give a formal speech without preparing for it?

It's not easy, but it can be done. If you're ever called upon to present a speech and you have only a few minutes to gather your thoughts, answer these five questions:

TIME: How much time am I given to speak?

MAIN POINT: What is the one main point I want to convey?

STORY OR ILLUSTRATION: Is there a story or illustration that I can attach to it?

STRONG OPENING STATEMENT: Is there a strong statement or question I can open with?

CONCLUSION: Can I conclude by coming back to the opening with a statement, question, benefit or an appeal?

The Ceremonial Speech

The ceremonial speech is given on special occasions: inaugurations, toasts, award or recognition presentations, award acceptances, eulogies, and dedications.

If you are accepting an award or recognition, finding just the right words — sometimes without preparation —can be a challenge. If you are presenting an award, it's important that you take the time to know how to pronounce all the names correctly. For example, write them phonetically on your notes.) Whatever form of ceremonial speech you're giving, be sure to be sincere and uplifting.

A Toast

A toast is a short speech that honors the moment. The toast has long enjoyed an important place in international diplomacy. It is a sentiment, a sign of respect, and a gesture of friendship. It can be elegant with poetry. Some of the best toasts are simple, brief and to the point. Simple and sincere are the words that best describe a toast. Thinking about a toast beforehand is a good idea. You really don't have to prepare or rehearse excessively.

An example of a short, effective toast is: *"To good health, friendship, and peace!"* Or to quote Mark Twain, *"May you live forever, and may the last voice you hear be mine!"* Or it can be as simple as one word which means either long life or good health.

The Political Speech

The four-part structure of a political speech is: <u>who</u> you are, <u>what</u> you stand for, <u>why</u> you are running for office, and <u>why</u> people should vote for you.

A "Stump" speech is an all-purpose speech that is repeated over and over again to different audiences. Hopefully it is refined to the point of perfection. The purpose of a Stump speech is for the audience to get to know the candidate, to like the candidate, to agree with the issues, and — most important! — to vote for that candidate.

The question of "why are you running for office?" should be answered in a single sentence. When you are asked, "Why should I vote for you?" your answer should be in *two* parts —

1)Your excellent qualifications, background and experience
2)Your ideas, creative thinking and plans for change

Remember to keep to your time allotment, to maintain good eye contact with your audience, and to smile and have a friendly demeanor. And always remember to ask for their votes!

An Emcee/ Master of Ceremonies

The Emcee or Master of Ceremonies is the host, the glue of the program. You must know the agenda, keep the flow of the
event going in a timely manner, improvise if there are problems or interruptions and never leave the podium unattended.

Executive Briefings

Briefing program managers host executives from other companies that may want to do business with each other. These meetings have become a common practice for many Fortune 1000 companies. They bring decision makers together for building business relationships.

The briefing manager sets up the meeting, arranges all of the details, and conducts the meeting itself. The briefing manager must make sure all of the issues are brought to the table, and must conduct the meeting in a way that alliances and business relationships are encouraged. The briefing manager is a combination of meeting planner, logistic arranger, diplomat and moderator — all rolled into one.

Facilitating, Training, Coaching, Consulting

Workshops or seminars are arranged when a company needs to solve problems, train employees, bring changes to the employees, move to a different environment, and build teams. When it is faced with strategic planning, restructuring the organization, or making major policy changes, a different type of speaking session is necessary.

Facilitating, training, coaching and consulting are all forms of speaking. In these sessions, a greater in-depth needs analysis is required. Facilitators must do more listening as speaking.

Facilitating and coaching are done in a workshop format. The facilitator and coach are able to monitor the change in behavior and attitudes of the participants. They gauge the positive results and see the behavioral changes.

Personal coaching is usually conducted one-on-one. When I coach executives who need greater communication and speaking skills, I am able to measure the progress as I work with them. Watching their growth to more powerful and confident leaders with stronger body language and speaking skills gives me a great deal of satisfaction.

THE FOCUS AND PURPOSE OF YOUR SPEECH

OK, it's happened. You have been invited to speak to a group. You should feel flattered — your audience presumes you have something worth sharing with them. Your responsibility now is to make sure that you *do* have something to say.

Your first order of business is to focus on identifying your audience so you can understand their needs and the information that they will be looking for. How do you do this? First, contact the person who asked you to speak. Ask as many questions as you can about the group that you will be addressing. What information and results are they looking for in your presentation?

Then seek out support materials pertaining to your audience. Some good sources are newsletters, brochures, annual reports, trade newspapers and the Internet. I also send questionnaires to the attendees beforehand to define their needs. This is an excellent method of getting your audience involved even before your presentation begins.

You can also speak to the managers, the customers, and the meeting planner. You can request the company newsletter, orientation manuals, product manuals, and statements that relate to the company mission, philosophy and target market. I also ask for the names of key people in the organization. The program chairman is usually happy to provide those names to the speaker. If you have acquired information from members of the audience, recognize them in your presentation and thank them for their assistance.

Once I was asked by the meeting planner to present a program on motivation and leadership. After questioning the managers and CEO of the company, I found that what they really wanted was a program on teamwork and internal customer service. To be effective you must talk to a lot of people and ask a lot of questions. In that way you can zero in on their requirements

If you are asked to address an organization that is not familiar to you, your best intentions won't save you from failure if you arrive uninformed. You are doing a disservice to your audience and to the meeting planner who hired you. Remember: the more you know in advance, the less that will be left to chance.

Although I encourage you to speak whenever possible, if you are asked to speak on a topic that is unfamiliar to you, I recommend that you decline the invitation. You might not be able to learn everything in a short period of time that others have taken years to learn. You don't want to get in front of a group until you know your program material thoroughly.

Here's a tip you might not have thought of, always check any publicity that the meeting planner distributes about you or your program and make sure everything is correct. I was once asked to present a 30-minute speech titled: "How to Succeed in Life Through Networking," and I prepared a terrific networking program for them.

When I arrived at the auditorium, the room was filling up with people. Soon there was standing room only! I thought, "My heavens, they must have heard what a good speaker I am," and "Wow, the next time they'd better rent a stadium." I asked the meeting planner, "Do you always have such a large attendance?" and she replied, "This is an unusually big turnout. In fact it is the largest crowd we have ever had. It must have been the topic."

I asked, "Can I see the publicity that was sent out?" She handed me the flyer (which I hadn't seen before) that was sent to the membership. Printed across the top of the flyer, in big, bold letters, was the title — "How to Succeed in Life Through NOT Working!"

You can imagine how I had to re-arrange my talk — on the fly — to win my audience's attention and respect

PREPARING YOUR SPEECH

The following is a checklist to help you acquire information on your speaking event and the questions to ask so that you can customize your presentation.

YOUR TOPIC

What is the topic of the speech?

What do you need to learn about the topic?

What materials and resources do you need for the required amount of time requested?

What are the specific objectives or results desired?

THE EVENT

What type of event is planned? (Seminar, keynote, panel, training)

What is the theme, objective, or occasion of the conference or meeting?

What is the date?

THE LOCATION

Will travel arrangements be involved?

Where is the event to be held?

THE AUDIENCE

What do you want your audience to know? Feel? Do?

Does your message fit your audience?

Is there value and benefit in your message?

Does your message apply to their industry? Their personal lives?

How informed are the attendees on the topic being presented?

How many people will be attending your session?

What demographics describe the attendees?

Do they pursue common occupations?

Do they work at different management levels?

What current challenges does their industry or association face? (Request examples)

What are the names and resources for further information? Who is the contact person?

What is the audience's attitude toward your topic? (interest, disinterest, hostility, anticipation)

Is the audience required to attend my session, or is it by choice?

Are there sensitive issues or topics that should be avoided?

THE PHYSICAL SETTING

How will the room be set up? (chairs, tables, auditorium)

Will I need props, audiovisual equipment, a screen, or a flipchart?

Is there a podium and lectern?

Can a Teleprompter be provided?

Will my presentation be recorded? If so, is it audio or video?

THE FORMAT

When am I scheduled to begin? End?

Are there other speakers on the same program?

What will take place prior to and immediately following my presentation?

Will there be a question-and-answer session following my speech?

Will a meal be served prior to or during my presentation?

May I promote or sell any products?

Does the program offer credit for continuing education?

Will I be paid an honorarium or fee?

When structuring your presentation, follow the format of: ***problems, causes, solutions, benefits.***

1) Introduction (Opening Remarks) + transition statement to lead into the main point
2) The Main Point + stories, illustrations, examples
3) The Second Point + stories, illustrations, examples
4) The Third Point + stories, illustrations, examples
5) The Benefits
6) Suggested Action
7) Closing Remarks
8) Questions From Audience
9) Final Close

Here's another suggestion. Keep a speaker's idea book. It is amazing how many ideas, quotes, stories, random thoughts and experiences you can jot down for future use. (It's also amazing how much you can forget if you don't write it down.) Ideas come out of the air at the most unexpected times. Don't say, "I'll write that down later." Choose it or lose it!

Joel Weldon, CPAE (Council of Peers Award for Excellence) and international speaker, asks, "Who really cares about what you have to say?" That's a good question. When you prepare your topic, keep asking yourself, "*who cares?*" Hopefully you can answer that question.

Customizing your material means focusing on "NFV" — Needs, Fears, and Victories. The research on your speech will make your presentation current and tailored to each audience. Check out industry buzzwords and terminology. Scattering such knowledge throughout your speech allows your audience to trust the information being presented.
  Some good sources for quick, reliable information include:

The U.S. Bureau of Census
The U.S. Department of Commerce
The Library of Congress
The U.S. Department of Labor

Trade and Professional Associations are eager to offer information. *The Encyclopedia of Associations* is available at your local library. It lists a description of every association in the United States.

http://www.Britannica.com — you can search through 76,000 articles

http://encarta.msn.com — free access to a concise encyclopedia of
        16,000 abridged articles and a world atlas

http://www.worldbookonline.com

http://www.funkandwagnalls.com — free encyclopedias and media gallery

http://www.infoplease.com — almanacs

http://www.internetoracle.com — search specialized encyclopedias

http://www.kalama.com — links to 40 encyclopedias and 60 dictionaries

http://www.libraryspot.com

http://www.refdesk.com

The Reverse Dictionary

The Wall Street Journal web site

The Celebrity Book of Lists

World's Greatest Speeches

The New York Times

Fortune magazine

I always ask the meeting planner to provide me with names of people that will be attending my presentation. I like to receive about six or eight names because not everyone can be easily reached. I find that asking them questions is very helpful in designing my workshop because it gives me insight into the information that the audience wants to hear. These are the questions I ask:

What are the issues that are current in your industry?

What information (on my topic) would you like discussed?

What areas of my topic do you feel are critical and need priority?

What are the strengths of your company (or association)?

Have you been offered training previously?

Could you give me an example of a specific problem or challenge that you have encountered?

How was it resolved?

ORGANIZE A SIMPLE STRUCTURE FOR A WELL CRAFTED SPEECH

The three main elements used to organize and present your speech — the OPENING (also called the grabber), the BODY (the main points), and the CLOSE (a summation of your main points).

Although I present my speech as opening-body-close, that is not the order in which I typically write it. I usually begin my preparation by writing the body of the speech, specifically the important points.

After I have written the body of the speech, I go to the close — sometimes this is an appeal, a summary, a call to action, or a statement of benefits.

It might surprise you that the last thing I write is my opening. I do this for a reason — this way I know where I am going and where I want to end *before* I begin.

Let's look at those three components of your speech, in the order that you will probably develop them. That means that we start with the body of your presentation.

The Body - The Main Objective

This portion of the speech should cover ninety percent of your presentation. Writing the body of your speech is straightforward. First you need to list the important points that you want to cover in your presentation.

After determining the points you want to cover, attach a story or illustration to underscore each point. The structure of the body of your speech will follow this formula:

• Make a point, then give an example, tell a story or show an illustration.

You can't just throw your points, one after the other, at your audience. Each point must have a transition to help the audience bridge from one point to the next. Otherwise, your points will be disjointed and your audience will be confused.

This is an example of a transition: "We have discussed (point 1) and that leads us to…," or "now we will follow that point with (point 2)." Transitions are very important to the flow of the speech.

Transitions help your audience follow the flow of your program. It helps even more if your points are presented in some sort of logical order. For example, your main points may be presented in chronological order, such as: "Fourscore and seven years ago…." (past), followed by, "Now we are engaged in a great civil war…" (present), finishing with, "…that this nation, under God, shall have a new birth of freedom" (future).

You can arrange your points by emphasizing their geographical relationship, or logical sequence, as a list of problems with their solutions, or even challenges and actions to be taken. Any order is acceptable, as long as it helps your audience to follow the flow of your program.

FIND YOUR HIDDEN CREATIVITY

You are creative! In fact, we are all creative. It's just that most of us don't realize that we have that capability. So now that you have assembled your research and profiled your audience, you are ready to create your speech. What better way to create a speech than to be creative!

Traditionally, we were taught in school to prepare a speech in outline form. That, however, is a most uncreative method. Outlines inhibit you, restrict your thinking, and keep you boxed into a format. And when you sit down to write your speech, you find that the ideas don't flow and you become anxious.

The best method I've found of freeing up your ideas or thinking out of the box is Mind Mapping™.

Have you ever noticed how and when good ideas enter your brain? They seem to spring out of nowhere. You could be anywhere — walking down a street, staring into space, or taking a shower. That is the kind of creativity flow that Mind Mapping allows you to tap into.

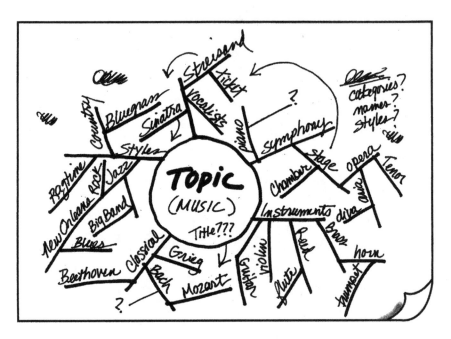

It's easy to do. Begin with a blank, unlined sheet of paper. Draw a circle in the middle of the page and write your topic in the circle. Now begin to add any thoughts that occur to you about that topic, using arms that stretch out from the circle for each idea that pops into your head. When one idea has numerous thoughts, add branches to the arms.

Don't be concerned with neatness. Don't worry about logic. Don't be particularly serious. Realistic or not, pertinent or trivial, silly or important — write all your ideas down. Often your best ideas will appear at first glance to be the least logical. Use colored pens.

When you're finished, your paper should look like a busy hodgepodge of lines and branches. But before you know it, your mind map will be a springboard for your speech's structured outline.

The next step is to decide how many points you wish to present. Many factors determine the number of points you should have in your speech. These factors include the length of your speech, the sophistication and depth of your points, as well as the educational and managerial level of your audience. In determining the length of your speech, remember that most audiences have about a forty-minute attention span — or less.

I'm sure you'll discover that Mind Mapping has many uses. I have used mind mapping for problem solving, speech writing and just everyday fun. I have used it in my workshops with fifty people working together on one map, and I have created small groups within a big crowd for team building and brainstorming exercises.

One of the best things about Mind Mapping is that it's easy to do, and there are not a lot of rules about doing it. Jim Barber of The Barber Shop (see Resources page), one of the most creative individuals I have ever met, states "The best environment for creativity is one where you are not hampered by unnecessary rules and restrictions."

No one is grading you on your creativity efforts. Jim also says, "Creative people view 'failure' positively as 'a good try' rather than something to be avoided and feared." So pick up a pencil or colored pens and start Mind Mapping!

DEVELOPING YOUR TOPIC

There are many avenues to help you develop your material. Of course, the Internet is a terrific place to start. However, I find going to the bookstore and checking out everything that is current on the topic is also important.

Conducting interviews with employees of the company or members of the association is an invaluable technique. Many speakers spend days walking around a corporation's headquarters, attending meetings and asking questions of employees on every level.

It is important that you stick to your field of expertise. Don't talk to bankers about banking unless you are also a banker. The same goes for every field. YOU can — and should — speak on the topic of your expertise.

Because I am a professional speaker, I have presented workshops on speaking skills to bankers, doctors and engineers. I have trained managers, business owners and employees on customer service. I have cutting edge effective training programs that produce results. I developed powerful networking skills that really work. I put all these techniques into a workshop format and presented them to sales professionals. They were good at sales, but they did not know networking techniques. After my workshop, they experienced a major improvement by expanding their spheres of influence.

What is *your* area of expertise? And if you are not yet an expert, what is the topic or life experience that is burning a fire within your soul? What information have you learned that you want to share with the world? What do you know that can be helpful to others?

But knowing what you want to talk about isn't enough. You need someone who wants to listen to you. Ask yourself if your topic is relevant to people's wants and needs. Will it improve their lives? Who will your target audience be? You need to understand the demographics, skills, educational levels, values, attitudes, interests and ages of your potential audience members.

And then, you must answer these four questions. It is what your audience is thinking.

1) What's the point?
2) So what?
3) Who cares?
4) Now what?

ADD SPICE WITH HUMOR AND STORIES

"I like to make people laugh so they take my message seriously."
— unknown

Humor embraces your audience and it helps to build an instant rapport with them. It allows the audience to feel like they are there to enjoy themselves. When an audience enjoys a speech, they are more apt to remember it, learn from it, and be motivated by it. Humor can be used effectively, even if your topic is serious or technical. It can relax your audience when tension builds or "techno talk" gets heavy. Remember that humor must always relate to the content of your speech

I have never been particularly successful telling a joke from the platform. I can, however, relate personal experiences that happen to be funny. Self-deprecating stories about mistakes I've made are often met with laughter from the audience. A little self-deprecating humor allows your audience to see you as one of them instead of as a perfect person who cannot possibly relate to them or their problems.

Of course, your humor must be authentic. I recommend that you keep a journal of your own stories and humorous incidents that you can refer to at a future date. Personalize the stories and adapt them to the event.

Great sources for humor include real life experiences, embarrassing moments, bumper stickers, quotations and cartoons. I found this philosophical statement on a T-shirt: "I'm retired! That means I have seen it all, done it all, know it all, and I have the time to tell it all."

Andy Rooney, television commentator on CBS's "60 Minutes," relates stories about the folly and irony of life that we can all relate to. He once said, "If you make a half-hour speech, it takes about three weeks — a day to get there, a day to get back, a couple of days to prepare it… and several weeks to worry about it." Funny, but with an element of truth to it!

Sometimes, despite your best intentions, your attempt at humor does not translate to your audience. In other words, "it bombs." For a quick remedy, you can always say, "I won't send that one to Jay Leno," or "Well, my mother thought it was funny."

Stories are a terrific way to deliver humor to your audience. They should have a rhythm and should flow. They should be short and not over labored.

Stories build tension, and then release tension. But remember, your stories, like all your humorous remarks, must have relevance and be germane to the message. The right stories can drive your audience to action. You can touch their heart. The best stories are your own and it gives the audience an opportunity to know you. Practice your stories in everyday conversation. If they don't work- drop them. Follow your story with a transition back to the point you are making in your speech.

Whatever its form, your humor should have a clear, unmistakable punch line. And be sure to allow a moment for laughs. Stories, word pictures, and self-disclosure all bring your points home. They warm the audience to you and allow them to relate to you as another human being.

Whatever experience you choose to share, avoid using clichés to bridge to your stories. Some of them make me cringe, like, "A funny thing happened on my way over here..." or "You have probably heard this one before..." or "I don't know if I can remember the punch line but...."

James Thurber, once said, "Humor is emotional chaos remembered in tranquility." It gives us the opportunity to reflect and laugh at ourselves and our human fragility. It is also one of the most effective tools that you can use as a speaker.

One final, important point — Any humor offered from the podium must be appropriate and in no way offensive to your audience.

Jokes are a special form of humor. You must have a good memory to tell jokes. (I keep forgetting the punch line, which is why I don't tell jokes!) You need to have a good sense of timing. And keep it short — if your joke is too long, your audience loses interest. Finally, the joke must be one they have not heard before, otherwise your audience responds with, "Oh, that old joke."

Be extremely careful if you choose to target someone in your audience with your humor. I have seen occasions when it has worked, and it was a lot of fun. But I have also seen it have disastrous effects, causing anger and humiliation. One careless remark can turn your entire audience against you.

Oh, and by the way, don't laugh at your own humor. The few times that I have tried to tell a funny joke, I started laughing. Unfortunately, I couldn't stop laughing long enough to give the punch line. And the audience sat there thinking that their speaker was an idiot!

The same goes for getting too emotional and crying. It is o.k. to get glassy eyed and drop a tear or two, but weeping and sobbing will make your audience uncomfortable and you will have lost your control.

Telling stories is like painting a canvas. Stories bring life to all material. They bring the message home. Stories motivate, they make the points real, and they are entertaining. Best of all, they help the audience remember your message.

Many speakers have a signature story— material that is unique to just that speaker. I have two or three such stories and I add them to almost all of my presentations. They help the audience get to know me. They are self-depreciating, true experiences.

When you think of your own signature story, you will want to practice it until it's perfect. I have told my signature stories so many times, I know when to pause for effect, just exactly where the audience will laugh, and the right gestures to use. A good signature story takes the audience on a journey.

Be sure to review your work! Once you have written the body, take a look at what you have created. Do the ideas flow easily from one point to the next? Do the stories and illustrations properly relate to the points?

Once you have the body written, it is time to proceed to the closing. Not the opening, that is written after the close.

The Close — The Finale — The Wrap up

Have you ever heard a speaker finish a speech… and the audience didn't know the speech had ended? The speaker just stands there, anticipating applause, and eventually the audience claps. That is a good way to lose any power or punch that the speech might have had.

Your closing is the last thing that your audience will hear, and quite possibly the easiest thing for them to remember. Don't waste such a great opportunity to make a lasting impression on your audience.

Close your speech with a strong conclusion. Tie all of your specific points together, summarize what you've said, make an appeal, a call to action, or a challenge. Remember to be uplifting and positive. Make it sound like a definite closing. It is trite to announce "… and now to end my speech" or "In conclusion…" After all, does a maestro say, "There are just a few more bars of music until the end"?

If you are ending your speech with a conclusion or a solution, be sure that you have adequately defined the issue or the problem. If you are ending with a call for action, your audience must be convinced there *is* a need or a reason to respond. And remember — never, *never* interject a new idea into the closing.

A good closing structure is like a circular staircase — it takes you back to the beginning, but at a higher level.

Use your wrap-up to ask for the order, summarize your main points, and leave the audience impacted. If you have a question-and-answer segment after your speech, prepare a *second* ending so that the audience knows that "this is really the end."

Be aware that even with the best planning and most rigorous rehearsal, the clock can run out before you reach your conclusion. Sometimes the previous speakers go over the allotted time or the event begins late. When this happens, skip the remaining points in your program and move to your conclusion, emphasizing the most important points that you have already stated. Don't tell the audience that you are omitting anything; you'll just make them feel as if they are missing important information.

Ending on schedule is good manners toward the audience, appreciated by the program chairman, and considered a professional standard. In order for you to keep track of your time, it is helpful if you can arrange for someone to give you a "last five minutes" signal. I also put my watch on the lectern. It has a big face with large numerals, and I can glance at it without anyone knowing that I am checking the time.

When you're finished, what do you do? A "thank you" at the end is optional, although it is discouraged by Toastmasters International. Their thought is that you don't need to thank your audience, and it takes away from the impact of your speech. Can you imagine Patrick Henry ending his strong emotional appeal, "Give me liberty or give me death. Thank you!"

The Beginning — Grab Their Attention

Now that you know where you have taken your audience, it is time to design the opening of your speech.

The beginning of your speech is the place to grab your audience's attention. It's the appetizer before the entrée. The opening of your speech welcomes your audience and alerts them that the main points are coming. The opening is important because it is at the beginning of your speech that your audience decides whether they want to listen or let their attention drift away.

The beginning is the point where you will either turn your audience on or turn them off. The first minute of your presentation will convince your listeners that the remaining minutes will be worth their time and attention. Consequently, you want to build that bridge with your audience immediately.

What do you say in your opening? When you begin to speak, it is only good manners to briefly thank the person who introduced you. Since the audience is receptive and expectant, don't crush that feeling with apologies

49

or statements that work against you, such as "I really don't know why they chose me," or "I didn't have time to prepare," or "This is not a topic that I know too much about."

I know the opening of my speech is important. Although I never memorize my speeches, I do know my opening lines by heart. That makes it possible for me to maintain good eye contact during those first important moments.

There are many things you can do to get your audience's attention. You can startle, jolt, and awaken them right at the start. Here are some excellent openings:
- A probing question
- A strong statement
- A reference to this date in history
- A personal story
- A news item or any story that is current and relevant to your message
- A quote that relates to your topic

Some final advice on openings: Stay away from the tired opening that begins with "I'm here to talk to you about...." Also, beginning with a joke — especially one you don't know very well — can be a disaster.

The opening should take your audience directly to the point of your speech in a creative, enticing way. The bridge between your opening statement and the body of your speech can be your opportunity to show the audience where you will take them next. Tune into their expectation. Make the journey an adventure.

A TITLE CAN TANTALIZE AND TEASE

Your speech title deserves a lot of thought. The title is the part of your speech that is similar to an invitation you receive in the mail. It can be inviting, interesting, have pizzazz and arouse interest. It can ask a question, state a fact, be elusive, or offer a promise. The title can build to the main point of the speech and be referred to in the summary. It can create a theme that is part of the whole event. It can entice and tantalize — as long as it relates to your message.

Create a title with sparkle. Rather than "Learn Speaking Skills," use "Speak with Power, Poise and Purpose." Instead of "How to Make a Speech," use "Your Turn at the Lectern." Whenever possible, try using three words with the same first letter to attract attention — "Define, Decide and Direct" or "Coffee, Cookies and Cream."

Ronald Reagan's farewell address was titled, "We Have Made a Difference." He proceeded to outline all of his accomplishments from the beginning of his eight years as President of the United States. After he reviewed all of his economic and global victories, he concluded his speech with "My fellow Americans, WE DID IT — we made a difference." That had impact!

The purpose of the title is to suggest the content, provoke curiosity, and arouse the interest of the audience. Be clever, but not coy. A number of years ago, I used a title for a motivational speech that I thought was unique. The material of the speech dealt with how we hold ourselves back and sabotage our success. The title was "Stop Dancing Backwards." No one was able to understand how the title related to the material. I quickly dropped it.

One last thing — although the title is very important, don't feel you have to create the title before you write your speech. You can come up with a title whenever inspiration strikes you.

USE NOTES THAT ARE EASY TO READ

Unless you have an excellent memory, don't try to memorize your speech. I often tell people that I have a photographic memory, but sometimes I forget to put the film in. Therefore, I never memorize speeches. Instead, I prepare very simple notes. If your speech is written out in full text, and you use that as your notes in your presentation, you will find that your tendency will be to read your speech. Perish the thought! You do not want to be tethered to a script. I can almost guarantee that your speech will be ineffective if you simply read it, word for word.

Many speakers use 3 x 4 or 5 x 7 cards for their presentations. Personally, I think cards are awkward. Speakers often lose their place and start shuffling them, which is quite noticeable to the audience. If you feel you must use cards, be sure that they are numbered and use only one side. I once saw a perfectly groomed, dressed-for-success speaker take a rumpled paper from his pocket and began to flatten it out!

Here's what I suggest: take your primary outline and create a *new* outline that uses just a few keywords for each point or story you intend to relate. Try to place this on one sheet of paper with a large bold font that can be easily read. Of course, it is important that you rehearse and present from that *second* outline.

I also highlight my outline with different colored pens to indicate where to use my overhead transparencies, a prop, or flipchart, or even schedule a coffee break. If you do this, use firm 20 lb, white paper that won't roll or curl. I use a slashes (//) to denote a pause and an insert symbol (^) for special emphasis. A red star indicates an audience participation exercise (see illustration). I phonetically write out any words that are difficult to pronounce.

SYMBOLS ON NOTES

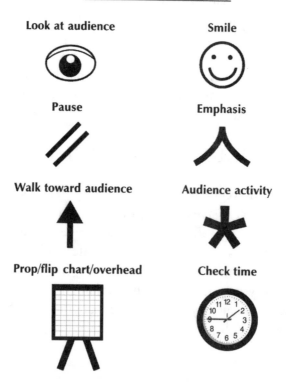

Look at audience

Smile

Pause

Emphasis

Walk toward audience

Audience activity

Prop/flip chart/overhead

Check time

If you make revisions on your notes, be sure to add some additional rehearsal time so that you feel comfortable with your notes. There have been times when I have looked at my unrehearsed notes and found they resembled hieroglyphics.

If your notes consist of a couple of pages, don't staple them. They won't turn easily. Be sure to number your pages. They have been known to drop on the floor, and numbered pages can be more quickly reassembled.

Here's another word of warning. Don't place your notes on the lectern in advance! They could be picked up by the previous speaker or the person giving your introduction. This has happened to me more than once.

If you are presenting technical
> **Material that must be read,**

You will find that if you
> **Stagger your sentences**
>> **Your eye will pick up**

Groups of words at one time and allow
> **more direct eye contact**
>> **with the audience.**

Use a 16- or 18-point font so the groups are easily seen. You will see the information in groups of words, and you will not sound like you are reading the text. If there is information you must read, use a conversational tone in your voice, use inflections, pauses, vocal variety and gestures. Make sure that your notes are not stapled.

I rarely use a lectern, because it creates a barrier between me and the audience. However, you can use a portable folding music stand (purchased at a musical instrument store). I set it up in the front of the room before I am introduced. The stand is unobtrusive, and holds my notes perfectly. I also have room on the stand to set my small travel clock. All of these are in clear view, and I can easily glance at my notes and check on the time.

If you prepare well and rehearse thoroughly, your notes will keep you on track and will be a blessing if you "go blank." One glance, and you know the sequential order of your speech. The best part is your audience will never even be aware that your notes are in front of you.

Here's an example of how I might write my one-page "key word" notes for an hour-long program:

KEY WORD NOTES

OPEN
NETWORK STORY

(This is my opening story on networking)

RISK

(Lead into 1st point — taking a risk)

SKIRT STORY

(My story — describing risk taking)

CHALLENGES

(Second point — the risk of challenges)

BENEFITS

(Benefits of taking challenges and risks)

PROCESSES

(Methodology of risk taking)

AUDIENCE SHARE

(Audience share risk experiences)

QUESTIONS

(Questions from audience)

ENDING — YEAR 2000 STORY
Closing story

What do you do if you forget your notes, lose them, or they just disappear? First of all, DON'T PANIC! It won't help. I know. I've tried it, panicking doesn't make things better at all.

Instead, if you take a moment to think about it, you will probably remember far more of your speech than you expect. So take a sheet of paper and write down a few key words that remind you of the opening, the main points, the stories, and the close. After all you did prepare it and rehearse it, so most of your speech will come back to you. Your presentation may even come off sounding more natural and spontaneous than if you hadn't lost your notes in the first place.

If there was detailed and technical information on your notes that you could not possibly recollect, tell your audience that life played a little trick on you, and you will send them detailed information later — but in the meantime, you will talk about the concept, the value and the benefits of your message.

PREPARE WORKBOOKS AND HANDOUT MATERIALS

Should you have handouts or workbooks to give to your audience members? Ask yourself these questions: *Will the handouts or workbooks be helpful to the audience? Will they support the key ideas and help the audience retain the information?*

Workbooks and handouts are excellent reinforcement tools that support the material you have presented. They give you the opportunity to offer an agenda page, which is appreciated by your audience. This is especially important if your material is technical, complex, or detailed.

Another benefit is that handouts free the participants from taking copious notes, and allow them to concentrate on your words. Workbooks also add value to your presentation. Of course, any handout material should be customized for the event with the date, location and client's logo printed on the front.

Materials can be given out either at the beginning or at the end of your program. The time you choose will depend on whether or not you want your audience to fill in information as you progress through your program.

If you do hand out your materials at the beginning of your program, you may want to take steps to prevent the audience from reading through everything before you present your material. Otherwise the handouts become your competition. At times, I have placed the materials under the chairs and asked for a pledge that no one opens the book before the end of the session. This works only half of the time. If I decide to hand out material at the end of the session, I advise my audience at the beginning so that they can relax and not worry about notes.

Your handout material should be easy to read with a uniform font. Provide double spacing and wide borders for notes. Create your master copy on white or ivory paper, or the copies will look shaded. Also, be sure to number your pages. You can then easily move between different pages during your presentation.

The best time to design workbooks, handout sheets, and reference materials is while you are planning your presentation. It is a nice idea to personalize the title page of your handout with the name of the client, event or theme of the meeting or conference. Also your audience will appreciate a list of resources on the back page.

You can present your materials in a variety of formats. I prefer spiral binding for notebooks because they lie flat. For long seminars or ongoing classes, I use a three-ring notebook with a clear plastic pocket on the front cover and spine. I then slip my own customized cover on the front. Three-ring notebooks are also convenient because pages of material can be added to the notebook during the seminar. It is also a nice idea to distribute your handout sheets in a file folder that can be filed as opposed to tossed out.

If you are sending your handout material to be copied by your client or shipping it to the meeting place, be sure to carry the original with you. From my experience, packages have been known to get lost, and it isn't fun tracking a package that was supposed to arrive yesterday in Chicago and is sitting in a warehouse in Detroit.

The benefits of providing worksheets include:

Provides more information than an overhead transparency and is easier to read.

Allows the audience to listen and not be tied to note taking.

Saves time when material is too detailed to cover in the time allotted.

Provides additional sources of information/references.

Gives the perception of added value and credibility.

Gives you an opportunity to put your name and a bio in front of the audience.

Serves as an ongoing reference, which enhances retention of the material.

HOW TO REHEARSE YOUR SPEECH

The better rehearsed you are, the more confident you will be. The better rehearsed, the less nervous. The better rehearsed, the more polished! If you try to wing it, you could get caught in the branches. Trust me. I've seen it happen more than once.

Some speakers rehearse in front of a mirror. That doesn't work for me. I find I am distracted by staring at myself in the mirror. I also find it difficult to rehearse in front of just one person (even if that one person is me). When I do, I become too focused on that one set of eyes, and I feel self-conscious.

So what do I do? I'll admit, I have a very unorthodox method — I line up chairs in my office, and I place teddy bears on the chairs! How did I get teddy bears in my office? I stole them from my grandson, and I won't return them. Besides, he's a teenager now, so he doesn't even remember them.

I have found that these bears make a terrific audience. Their large button eyes offer good eye contact. Some of them are even smiling. It's true, they don't give me a standing ovation — but hey, it beats talking to lamps. I turn on my tape recorder, and away I go.

After you have audio taped your presentation, play it back to check your timing, your voice level, your phrasing, and your level of enthusiasm. Then make revisions and rehearse it again. Soon you will notice improvement in your presentation.

Recording yourself provides you with an endless source of self-analysis. Do you worry that the recording doesn't sound like you? Forget it. Everyone says that when they hear themselves on tape.

As you rehearse, keep in mind that timing is important. If you are asked to speak for 30 minutes and you end after 20 minutes, your audience and the meeting planner may feel cheated. They might ask, "Did you run out of things to say?" On the other hand, if you go over 30 minutes, the same people might get irritated.

You don't have control over everything. You may have prepared and rehearsed a 30-minute speech — but when you arrive, they inform you that you will be speaking for just 20 minutes. (This is not an unusual occurrence.) Don't panic and don't complain. Just cut part of your speech. Remember that the program chairman has a schedule to maintain. Also, your audience will get restless if you speak longer than they expect, especially if it is lunchtime or at the end of the day.

To give you a rough idea on timing, reading one page of text usually averages about one minute thirty seconds. This obviously depends on how fast you speak and the format of your notes.
When you tape your rehearsal, you will be able to better estimate your speech's timing.

When you read your text, whether silently or out loud, you'll generally find that the time runs much quicker than when you present your speech in front of an audience. So plan accordingly.

Practice cutting and switching your material and adjusting your notes to be flexible. This will help you prepare, should you run out of time. On the other hand, be prepared with additional material just in case you zip through your prepared speech... only to discover that you still have ten minutes to go. It's tough to stand up and do a tap dance until your time is up. Be sure that your rehearsal includes any visuals, overheads, props or flipcharts. Also, build in time for audience interaction.

Professional speakers rehearse standing up. If you do this, you will find your energy level increases, and so will your enthusiasm. Standing up also enables you to practice your moves from the lectern to the projector, or from your flipchart to the audience.

Anticipate parts of your presentation that might generate questions from your audience, and make a list of possible questions or challenges that might arise. Preparing answers to these questions will show that you are very knowledgeable. Spend most of your time rehearsing your opening remarks, the key points, the transitions and the close.

The American manned space program used a term called "adapting out." This is a technical way of saying "learning by repetition." The first astronauts repeated simulations over and over again. This repetition of experiences that they might encounter in space gave them the confidence that they would be faced with very few surprises.

That is also a comfortable way to feel when you are making a presentation. So keep rehearsing until you can say with confidence:

I know this material.

I know the sequential order of my points.

I know the transitions between my points.

I have memorized my opening and closing remarks.

I have rehearsed my stories.

I am comfortable with my notes.

I have some additional material "just in case."

I have planned and prepared for difficult questions.

My gestures work with my words.

My timing is on target.

I am authentic.

The more time you invest in practice and rehearsal, the more natural and spontaneous you will sound.

Whenever possible, I try to gain access beforehand to the room in which I will be presenting. Rehearsing my opening in that room makes me feel comfortable. If I am using audiovisuals, I like to know where everything is located. These are the things that will help you feel secure and confident. When the audience arrives, you will be ready.

Memorized speeches often sound "canned," but it is a good idea to memorize your KEY WORD notes. Don't memorize your entire speech, and NEVER, NEVER read your speech. Trying to memorize your material makes you a slave to your memory, and the material controls you. It doesn't sound conversational and natural. Your normal voice inflection changes and levels off to a monotone, and your expression and emotion are lost. Mother Teresa is the only person I've ever known who could read her speeches and be authentic.

Some people feel that no amount of preparation and rehearsal is enough. I always wish "If only I had more time" or "If only I had rehearsed a few more times." It's like preparation paranoia.

Is there such a thing as being over prepared? I think so. You do your best to prepare for the pitfalls (see Part 5) but if you attempt to memorize every word, you could come off sounding like a robot. Your mind will be busy covering the script and you will not be concerned with your audience.

Spontaneity is a charming attribute for a speaker. And that can come… as long as you are not trying to remember a script word for word. Preparation is important, but not over-preparation.

The key is rehearsal. You should rehearse to:

Memorize your opening sentence.

Know your main points.

Know the transitions from one point to the next.

Know your stories.

Know when to use visuals.

Prepare for difficult questions.

Memorize your closing remarks.

Practice for time.

Practice out loud.

Tape your voice.

If you can, do a videotaped rehearsal.

Practice standing up.

Practice looking at members of the audience. (You probably won't have an actual audience, so make "eye contact" with objects in the room — chairs, lamps, pictures, or teddy bears. Some people tie smiley-face balloons to chairs to create an audience.)

Practice smiling at your audience.

Are you using PowerPoint? If so, rehearse the order of the slides and the transitions between the sides.

It is different for everyone, but a good rule of thumb is: you should spend 25% of your time researching the material and the audience needs; 50% actually writing your speech, developing key issues, preparing handouts, and developing your KEY WORD notes; and 25% of your time rehearsing.

WRITE YOUR OWN INTRODUCTION

"It's strange to be 'introduced' by someone you have never met!"
— *Andy Rooney.*

Every speaker is entitled to an introduction. Only the President of the United States needs no introduction other than "Ladies and gentlemen, the President of the United States." Most professional speakers, however, prefer to write their own introductions. It is the only way they can be sure the information will be correct, and the right tone will be provided for their program.

As a rule of thumb, introductions should be brief, 30 to 50 seconds at the most. The goal of the introduction is to lead-in to your speech. Focus on points directly pertinent to why you have been asked to be a presenter. Also, don't overload on your credentials, family background, hobbies, or scholastic achievements. Be careful about adding too many superlatives, it will sound boastful and you don't want to lose credibility before you begin. In addition, NEVER USE OVERUSED AND SENSELESS PHRASES like "Without further ado" or "This speaker needs no introduction."
Dale Carnegie, professor and author of such classics as *How to Win Friends and Influence People*, offered this pattern for writing an introduction: **T. I. S. N.**

Topic (briefly explained)

Importance (or benefit to the audience)

Speaker's qualifications

Name of speaker. Your name should generally be the last thing mentioned in your introduction. It is the signal to the audience to applaud.
After you've developed your introduction, type it in a large bold font, double-spaced. If your name is difficult to pronounce, type it phonetically.

63

Send your introduction ahead of your speaking date to the person who will be introducing you, so they can practice it. (However, always bring an additional copy with you. Don't ask me why, but introductions often get lost or left behind in an office.)

Ask the person introducing you to read your introduction a few times to make sure he or she is comfortable with it. Request that he read it exactly as you have written it. Hopefully he will use a little expression and enthusiasm in his voice. I have heard my name twisted and mispronounced on several occasions, and I have not appreciated it.

Bill Gove, a great speaker and the first president of the National Speakers Association, had a great technique. He asked the introducer to end the introduction with, "And Bill, you must tell us your famous story about..." What a terrific lead-in to the story he wanted to relate!

On one speaking occasion, I was introduced after the announcement of the death of a cherished member of the organization. The introduction went something like, "Can we all stand for a minute of silence for our dear departed friend. And now, here is Carolyn Stein." The audience was sad before I began, and I don't think I changed their somber mood.

How should you begin your presentation? It is always good manners and perfectly proper to thank the person who introduced you. I know some speakers do not feel this is necessary, but I feel strange when a fine introduction has been offered and is not acknowledged. It appears rude.

Some speakers exude a lot of energy, and begin their speech before they even reach the podium. This can certainly generate excitement and anticipation. On the other hand, I feel that the audience needs a few seconds to focus on the speaker after the introduction. While either way works, the important thing is to find a style that works for you.

SAMPLE INTRODUCTION

Our speaker this morning, Carolyn Stein, is an Author, International Speaker and Chief Engineer of the Training Express, a customer service training company. She has presented these workshops on five continents to major corporations and Associations. She can say Pepto-Bismol in six languages and is always surprised when her luggage arrives with her. And now to put you on track to learn power speaking skills, I present to you...Carolyn Stein

GETTING ON AND OFF THE STAGE

You can't begin your presentation until you get comfortably in front of the audience. And sometimes that's not as easy as it sounds. Before you begin, notice the placement of the stairs, and determine where you will get on and off the platform. You don't want to look lost and confused before you utter your first words.

When you are introduced and you head for the stage, move with fast steps, energy and good posture. But don't run — you could sound breathless and be panting when you finally reach the microphone. Adjust the microphone, smile and sweep the audience with your eyes.

Instruct your introducer not to relinquish the stage until you arrive. You don't want to arrive at an empty stage. When you reach your introducer, you should immediately shake hands with him and acknowledge him and whoever is on stage. Now you're ready to begin your presentation!

When you have concluded your speech, accept your applause graciously. The audience wants to applaud your effort, so you should not run shyly off the stage. This would reduce your hard-won power and tarnish your professionalism. So recognize and accept the applause. When the introducer or another pre-selected person takes over the control of the podium, then you can walk briskly off the stage.

QUICK REVIEW

SPEECHES COME IN MANY FORMS

THE FOCUS AND PURPOSE OF YOUR SPEECH

SHOULD MATCH YOUR AUDIENCES' NEEDS

THE STRUCTURE: THE BODY - MAIN POINTS

CRATE A MINDMAP

USE HUMOR, STORIES, WORD PICTURES

THE CLOSE, WRAP UP

THE OPENING, A GRABBER

CHOOSE AN INTERESTING TITLE

USE NOTES THAT ARE EASY TO READ

PREPARE WORKBOOKS

REHEARSE

WRITE YOUR OWN INTRODUCTION

Part 3

STAGING THE EVENT AND SETTING THE SCENE

"The overture is about to start, you cross your fingers and hold your heart. It's curtain time and away you go — another opening of another show."

—From "Kiss Me Kate" by Cole Porter

STAGING THE EVENT
AND SETTING THE SCENE

THE ROOM ARRANGEMENT

You have been asked to speak. You have planned, prepared and rehearsed. You are ready, right? Wrong! There are a few more things to consider, such as the comfort of the audience and the comfort of the speaker. Attention to the physical arrangements of the presentation room, the chairs, the lights, the microphone, the temperature, the sound system, the audiovisual equipment — all these things have an impact on the success of your speech.

Most of the time, other people take responsibility for these things, so you can concentrate on your program. But in the final analysis, it is you, the presenter, who will benefit if everything is in order. Therefore, you should take the initiative to check these details. After all, your audience's comfort is crucial to your presentation's success.

Countless times, I have arrived at a speaking engagement to find the room in disarray, or not set up as I had requested. The room had insufficient chairs, or they were facing the wrong way. The lights were not bright enough, or the microphone did not work.

That's when I take off my jacket, roll up my sleeves, and move tables, chairs, the lectern, and the overhead projector. I put in a call for the building engineer to change the room temperature, adjust the lights, and connect the sound system. Once everything is in order, I am ready to set out my handout materials, organize my overhead transparencies, and rehearse my speech.

You will also find it very helpful to have a "room chairman" to help you when you first arrive. The room chairman will assist you in greeting the attendees, monitoring the door, and holding up a time signal to alert you when it is time to wrap up your program. The room chair can also give your introduction and distribute reference materials. If you have a large attendance, request the meeting planner (or the person in charge of your program) to arrange a room chairman.

The seating arrangement affects the way your audience experiences your presentation. The arrangement of the chairs in the room affects the format of your presentation and the rapport that you wish to establish with your audience. Classroom style seating with tables and chairs is the most comfortable for long sessions. Tables allow for easier note taking and provide a place for participants to rest their elbows.

I often request a chevron-shaped classroom style. The center aisle allows me to walk down the middle of the room and interact with the audience. In addition, I find this arrangement the most flexible for turning chairs around to form small breakout groups. Also, space between tables for an aisle allows attendees to leave the room without causing a distraction.

Auditorium or theater-style seating is usually most efficient for large groups, but the participants often don't like it as much. So if the rows are curved rather than placed in a straight line, you will establish a friendlier, more inclusive atmosphere. Straight rows inhibit interaction.

For small group discussions, the U-shaped table often works best. This configuration allows participants to see each other's faces, and everyone becomes part of the group. People often choose an elongated conference table, but this makes it difficult for some people to view the speaker.

Round tables are very effective for small group discussion, Mind Mapping, problem solving, or any team activity.

The chevron classroom-style puts the focus on the presenter. It also reminds adults of a school classroom.

The semicircle offers a warm group feeling.

A SEATING CHART

The seating arrangement contributes to the attention, interest, comfort and participation of the audience.

Classroom Chevron

Comfortable for workshops, the angle allows the participants to interact. Good for small to medium sized groups.

Banquet Rounds

Useful for small group break-out sessions. The drawback is that round tables encourage side conversations.

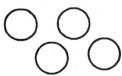

U-Shape

Open and informal Presenter can offer demonstrations easily.

Circle

Informal and open to interaction.

Auditorium

Used for large groups. Audience participation is limited.

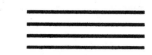

Boardroom

If the table is a long rectangle it is difficult for everyone to see the presenter.

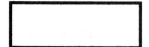

Squared-Off "U"

More adaptable than the square. Chairs can be placed both on the inside and outside of "U"

Semicircle

Not as intimate as a circle. Allows the leader to take charge.

Square

Formal and difficult to make eye contact.

Amphitheater

Better than an auditorium.

The squared-off "U" allows the presenter to move into the center and approach the audience.

The circle or the square does not offer space to comfortably utilize a flip chart or slides.

A large rectangular table is called conference or boardroom style. It is good for group problem solving. Everyone is facing each other and included in the group. However, it isn't flexible if you want to break the group into smaller discussion groups.

Because most rooms are rectangular, request that chairs be set up across the wide side of the room, if possible. Otherwise the room will resemble a bowling alley. A long narrow room places participants far away from the front and makes it hard to see and hear the presenter.

Here are some other thoughts. Always request that the chairs be positioned facing away from the door. This way, latecomers (or those who need to leave the room early) will not disrupt your presentation. The water or coffee station should also be located in the rear of the room. If it is possible, avoid interlocking chairs; they force people to be too close physically and there usually isn't enough elbow room.

Before my audience arrives, I navigate the room to see if the front of the room is clearly visible to everyone. If I'm using a screen or monitor, I look to see if it can be seen from all areas.

Vacant seats in the front or center of the room create "dead energy," something you want to avoid. Cordoning off the back rows will encourage participants to sit towards the front of the room. (Another alternative is to offer a 1st class "upgrade" to those who sit in the first rows.) As the audience enters the room, especially for a workshop, the middle and back fill up first.

Give thought to the fact that people in your audience might have special needs such as wheel chairs, hearing impaired or need to exit early.

Chairs should face away from the windows. Glare from the sun or outside activities will distract your participants. I learned this the hard way when I was presenting a workshop to a group of ten men at a country club hotel where the meeting room faced the pool. The session began at 8:30 A.M., and everything was working well. There was interest and participation from the group. By 10 A.M., however, none of the men were establishing eye contact with me. I turned around to discover all the attendees had focused their eyes on two women in bikinis sitting poolside. So at the morning break, I closed the drapes. (They hated me!)

Gather this information while your presentation is in the planning stage:

What is the size of the audience?

Is the room large enough to avoid crowding?

Can I avoid a small group of people in a large room?

Can the room be sectioned off?

Will there be group interaction?

Will the audience be writing, and will they need tables?

Do I want a formal or informal atmosphere?

Will I be using props and slides, a screen or video?

It is helpful to present a diagram of your room preference to the program chairman or meeting planner. Visit MediaNet's website (www.medianet-ny.com) to print out some diagrams of typical seating arrangements.

THE PROJECTION SCREEN

Request a matte finish screen for your projection activities. It provides the best horizontal viewing angle. Of course the screen should not be too low (the back rows need to have visibility) or too high (where everyone will have to strain their necks and chandeliers could obstruct the top of the screen).

A front-screen projection is the most popular setup, but AV experts will tell you that rear-screen projection produces better contrast ratios. Whichever you use, it is best if the screen is not directly behind the speaker where it competes for the audience's attention.

Here's a pet peeve of mine: if you are going to use one of those laser beam pointers, make sure it stays steady. Honestly, I have gotten seasick from watching those beams of light dance on the screen.

Finally, here's a very important point — NEVER turn your back to the audience to read off of the screen. I see this happen all of the time, and it's a certain way to lose your connection with the audience.

DOORS

Once the meeting gets underway you will find that latecomers, people leaving early, or people just walking in and out can be a huge distraction. To help counteract this, check the door before you audience arrives. If it doesn't close softly, put some duct tape over the latch to keep the door from clicking, squeaking and banging.

THE PODIUM AND THE LECTERN

Podium

The word podium is derived from the Greek word *podion* meaning *base*, and refers to a structure above the floor level. Podiums, or "risers," come in a variety of heights. If you are presenting to more than thirty people, and especially if you are short in stature, you may need a podium just to be seen. Those seated toward the back of the room will tend to lose interest if they cannot see you easily.

Using a podium presents its own problems. If the podium is too high, you will tower above your audience. You certainly don't want to look down at them because this can damage your effort to connect with them. Also, be sure to check the steps leading from the floor to the podium. Sometimes the stairs are only on one side.

Make sure that if you step down after addressing the audience, you can do so without stumbling. But if you do stumble you can always say, "I fall back in the fall, and spring forward in the spring" or to quote Tom Antion, "Give me an inch and I'll take a fall" or "Shall I try that entrance again?" Taking a humorous approach to your problems will help you recover, and will put your audience at ease.

Lectern

Traditionally, a lectern is a desk to support a book for a standing reader. It has a flat surface set at an angle. The word lectern comes from the Latin word *legere*, meaning *to read*. In the past, books and bibles were very large and heavy, and they required a special stand.

Lecterns are frequently used by speakers today to hold their notes. Unfortunately, it also can create a barrier between you and your audience. You will find lecterns tend to be large and overpowering, and they restrict your movement. Some lecterns are so big they can hide the presenter — especially if they're height-challenged like me. (I'm 5'2".) Consequently, I prefer to use a small music stand. It is unobtrusive, it holds both my notes and my clock, and it does not create a barrier between me and my audience.

There are many different types of lecterns — floor lecterns, table lecterns, adjustable clear plastic lecterns, and portable folding lecterns. In fact, the sound system for the room is sometimes built into the lectern. This can be convenient, but if you need a microphone and do not wish to stay behind the lectern, you must either carry a handheld microphone or wear a lava-liere.

Find out in advance how large the lectern is and if it will be set on a riser (podium). I can assure you that if the audience cannot see your face, your message will be lost.

It is really nice, after you become comfortable being in front of an audience, to step in front of the lectern, and bridge with the audience. Without notes in your hand.

This can happen to anyone. On an official visit to the United States, Queen Elizabeth was addressing an audience. Because she was standing behind a massive lectern, the only part of her that was visible was her hat. The headline under her photo said simply: "A talking hat." (If someone had provided her either with a small riser to stand on or a smaller lectern, this embarrassing incident could have been avoided.)

DON'T PUT YOUR AUDIENCE IN AN OVEN OR A FREEZER

Room Temperature

The room should be neither cold nor hot. Too often I've had to wrap my arms around myself to keep from freezing, or I needed to make a paper fan to avoid melting. Your audience will not appreciate freezing or frying.

To avoid these problems, see to it that the room temperature is between 68 and 72 F (20 to 22 C) during your program. (Remember that when you first enter an empty room, it will feel cooler. That will change, however, when the room fills up with people.) If you are not sure about the temperature, ask your audience. They will be happy to tell you if they are roasting or turning to ice. (Hopefully you discovered the name of the building engineer and where to locate him… before your program began.)

Using a Teleprompter

The Teleprompter can be a great aid to a speaker. It creates the impression that the speaker is looking at the audience. Actually, the speaker is reading from a script that's being displayed in front of the speaker, but is invisible to the audience. An operator scrolls the text according to the pace of the speaker. All the audience sees is a flat, clear Plexiglas stand.

Although Teleprompters can be powerful tools to use, it is crucial that you rehearse with one before using it. The type used for your script should be large and easy to read. You can even include symbols for pauses, smiles and emphasis.

Like any other equipment, however, a Teleprompter can fail or break down, the scroll with your speech on it can be misplaced, or the wrong scroll can be loaded. I have seen it happen at major conventions in front of thousands of people. So always, *always* have an extra copy of the script with you at the lectern.

The Microphone

If you haven't used a microphone before, it is not uncommon to feel a little intimidated by it. Some people actually have "micro-phobia," a fear that the amplified voice will be too loud and everyone will hear you breathe. True, if you use it improperly the microphone does pick up every sound — the rustling of your notes, your jewelry, taking a sip of water, the whooshing of a silk blouse or tie. Despite this, the microphone really is your friend.

A microphone is a huge aid in presenting a successful program. It eliminates the need to project your voice to the back of the room, and it keeps you from becoming hoarse and straining your voice. In fact, it can actually enhance your voice because you can use more vocal variety.

You have a number of choices when it comes to choosing a microphone — wireless or wired, handheld or lavaliere or attached to the lectern. I prefer a lavaliere wireless system that I attach to my lapel. The beauty of a lavaliere is that both of my hands are free to demonstrate, use a flipchart, or arrange overhead transparencies. And a wireless microphone enables me to walk around the room without tripping on a cord. (I've done that more than a few times!)

I also have the option of using a handheld wireless, which is great when I go into the audience and can offer the microphone to a participant. Handheld microphones are versatile, but you have to be careful to hold them in the correct position. If you keep the microphone four to six inches (the distance of two fists) from your mouth, the sound should be right. If it is too close, your lips will brush against it and create a blurring and slurring sound. Also, the letters p, t, s, and b will cause that breathy, popping sound that is unpleasant for the audience.

If you use a stationary microphone provided at the lectern, adjust it once and leave it alone. Some speakers get into the nervous habit of constantly adjusting the direction of the microphone every time they begin a new thought. You must make sure, though, that you speak into the microphone.

Maintain a constant distance from the microphone and speak toward it. This will avoid the sound from fading in and out.

Another important reason to arrive at your meeting room early is to test all your equipment before the audience arrives. Be prepared for unexpected technical surprises. An unpleasant squeal from your sound system is called "feedback," and it means that the sound from the speaker system is being fed back into the microphone and amplified again.

Feedback is not an unusual occurrence. When it happens to you, just move away from the microphone and turn down the volume. Don't let it break your concentration. When that happened one evening to a well known speaker, he looked at the audience and said, "Is there a spaceship arriving?" Everyone laughed and he continued with his program.

Feedback isn't the only microphone challenge you might encounter. What do you do when your microphone "goes dead?" Send for the engineer or a technician! And until they can fix the problem, speak as loudly as you can and pray the lights don't go out and the sprinkler system doesn't turn on Last year, that happened to me. My microphone stopped working and there was nothing that could be done. No engineer in sight. So in my loudest projecting voice I announced, "I speak about power, and it's just been cut off." I broke the audience into small groups, set up topics for each group to discuss, then walked around and addressed each group personally. It turned out amazingly well.

There are many advantages to bringing your own equipment. Having your own equipment means better control. Also, the equipment that the meeting facility provides is often merely adequate and not of the best quality. I prefer to use top-of-the-line equipment such as my Samson CT3L transmitter with a Samson MR-1 receiver and my wonderful Marantz tape recorder.

Whatever system you use, always remember to install fresh batteries before each appearance. Carry spare batteries with you. Weak or old batteries can die at any time.

Whenever you are presenting to a group out-of-doors, you always need a microphone. It may seem peaceful and quiet, but there are so many unnoticed sounds outside — planes flying overhead, passing cars, even the wind.

Of course, even when you prepare thoroughly and do everything right, the unexpected can still happen. For example, a few years ago I was giving a workshop to a group of expatriate women in Amboseli, Kenya, East Africa. The weather was perfect, so we set up chairs on the lawn of the Amboseli Lodge. I was using a good sound system provided by the lodge. What could possibly go wrong?

Actually, everything did go quite well… until we heard loud roars coming from the nearby woods. Within moments, a large herd of elephants came trampling toward us. I'd like to claim that it was something I said that attracted them, but the truth is, the elephants were not at all interested in what I had to say. We all fled immediately.

I never did find out what happened to the microphone.

As you can see, you have many choices when it comes to using a microphone. The most important decision is to use one when you need it. Be considerate of your audience — sitting in the back of a room, straining to hear a speaker is just not enjoyable.

LIGHTING THE ROOM

When you were a member of the audience, did you ever try to keep your attention on a speaker who was standing in a shadow? You lose your interest very quickly. So when you're the speaker, why make the audience strain to see you? If the audience can't see your face, your expression, and your eyes looking out at them, you put yourself at a big disadvantage.

Surprisingly, most speakers don't pay much attention to the lighting in the room, and that's a big mistake. Good lighting is a big help to any presentation.

It isn't only the stage that should be properly lit. If the light on your audience is too dark, you can't see their reactions to your words. Also, your audience will have trouble taking notes. On the other hand, if the light is too bright, the glare and intensity will fatigue your audience and become a major annoyance. Finally, look behind you — if the wall or curtain behind you is too bright, you will be backlit and your face will be in a shadow.

The stage as a whole may be well lit, but what about where you're standing? I have seen well-lit meeting rooms with the only dark spot directly over the lectern. If you ever have that situation, move the lectern!if the lights on you are too bright, the glare will irritate you and light hitting your eyes can be painful.

When you are using a projector, you should dim the lights. But not too low! If you make the room too dark, the result will be zzzzzzz's coming from the audience. If your audience starts to snore, turn on the lights as quickly as possible!

Checking the room lighting is another reason to arrive at the meeting site early. Start off by adjusting the room lighting. Most rooms have two types of light source — fluorescent light and incandescent light. Between the two, I prefer incandescent lighting. Fluorescent lights, while they illuminate the room, can be very overpowering. The tint from the harsh white light is not flattering, and the intensity cannot be adjusted; they can only be used at full brightness. Also, some fluorescent lights produce a low level buzzing noise which is often picked up on audio amplification and recording systems.

Incandescent lighting, the same kind of lighting you would typically have in your living room, is softer and gentler than fluorescent. Most incandescent lighting sources in meeting rooms have a dimming control that will allow you to set an ideal intensity level.

When using an overhead projector, keeping 50 percent of the house lights lit is generally enough. Often it is possible to ask the hotel staff to remove one light bulb directly above the screen, and this helps matters even more.

During playback of video monitors, darken the room to about 20 percent. The projection screen should be angled so that the entire audience can have an unobstructed view, Of course, this is true for any and all visuals.

Most auditoriums have a bright "whitewash" of floodlights on a stage area. Although this does light the stage, it also overpowers the audience and the speaker, and it may detract from the impact of your presentation. By using focusable lighting instruments called ellipsoidal spotlights (leko lights, as they are commonly known), you can light the stage area in segments. This will allow you to darken the light shining onscreen when you are using slides or overhead projectors… but still maintain light on you, the speaker. You can even warm the stage by asking for colored gels to cover the lights. Soft amber or a light rose are the most flattering colors to use.

The location of these lighting instruments is also important. If you place the lights in the back of the room, you will be blinded by the light hitting you head-on. So position the lights on the sides of the room, about one-third to halfway down the room from the stage, so that the light hits you at an angle of approximately 45 degrees from both sides of the room. The existing room light that you have already set with the dimmers will provide enough fill light to ensure that you do not look "flat."

In additions to these basics, many varieties of lights and special effects can be used to highlight a product, emphasize a point, or dramatize your presentation. Most of the time, the meeting planner or the building engineer will take charge of the room lighting. It is just a good idea for you to be aware of the effect of light on your presentation. Remember, proper lighting will keep the attention focused on you.

MUSIC

Background music can turn an ordinary meeting into a memorable event. When participants enter the room, music can set the mood for your program. Dynamic music will invigorate and wake up a sleepy audience. Exit music can have them dancing out of their seats as they head for the next session.

Resources for Organizations sells prepackaged copyright-free music that is appropriate for meetings. (See Resources) If you choose to use copyrighted music, you must get the appropriate licensing. Check with your meeting planner to see if they have an agreement with ASCAP (American Society of Composers, Authors, and Publishers). You certainly don't want to have your client — or yourself — involved in a lawsuit.

VISUAL AIDS — ADDING REALISM TO YOUR WORDS

Introducing visual elements during your presentation increases your audience's attention. Visual aids bring life to your presentation, and many options are available to you as a speaker or trainer — from the old faithful flipchart to computer-driven videos.

I find a good old-fashioned flipchart works well for small group training. Most meeting rooms provide an easel, so you may not feel that you need to own one. They are a bit bothersome to transport, but if you do purchase your own easel, make sure that it is sturdy.

Use a lined easel pad with a perforated top for easy removal of the pages. The lines keep the printing straight. When writing, keep your letters at least three inches high for maximum visibility. Be sure to use markers that don't bleed color through to the next page and squeak when you write. (I use Sanford Flip Chart Markers). Studies have shown that color is 20 percent more persuasive than simple black and white. However, avoid using the pale colors (pink or yellow). They are too light to be easily seen.

Whenever possible, I prepare my sheets in advance, using colored markers to highlight important points. I keep a blank sheet in between each page of material so that when I am done with one, the next page is hidden until I want to display it. I use small tabs to indicate each page's contents, and I write notes to myself on the side in pencil. (I can see these lightly penciled notes, but my audience cannot.)

Before you begin, make sure that your pad fits your easel. Some easels use a clamp on the top to hold the pad and others have hooks. I found out the hard way that not all pads fit every easel.

Flip charts can be placed anywhere in the room. You can tear off the pages and post them on the walls with masking tape. (Ask permission to use tape on the walls.) Flip charts don't work for a large audience, so you should turn to a larger format such as overhead transparencies, video and PowerPoint.

Slides and overheads are a powerful tool for speakers and trainers to use. However, avoid becoming dependent on them. Don't use them in place of notes for your speech. They should be used as support, not as your script.

Prepare your slides and transparencies so that they are easy to read. Use the 1 – 6 – 6 rule — no more than one idea per visual, six lines per visual, six words per line. Use both upper and lower case letters (using all capitals is tiring to read) and your text should be at least one inch in height. Hewlett Packard and 3M will send you free information on how to design overhead transparencies, and the information is also appropriate for computer-generated slides.

What font should you use on your slides? Sans serif and Arial black fonts are usually the best choice. Avoid mixing too many different fonts. You want the audience to focus on the words not the lettering..

You can format your material in different ways — italicize, bold, bullets and boxes — to make important points stand out. (However, you should avoid underlining because underlined words are hard to read.) Choose a text color that contrasts with the background. The font size should be about 40-point for titles and 30-point for text. Never go below 20-point for text; it becomes hard to see from the back of the room Limit the text on your slide to a few key words. Your slide is an aid for you and your audience — it is not your speech!

Finally, if you are mixing graphics or illustrations with your text, place the type to the left of the illustration. People are accustomed to flush left and ragged right copy (unless it is in Chinese, Arabic or Hebrew).

If you're using transparencies, run through a rehearsal with them to make sure they are in the correct order and are right side up. Arrange to have a table nearby on which to keep all your transparencies. This will prevent the distraction of them falling all over the floor. However, if they should fall, you can easily reassemble them... if they are numbered
I prefer cardboard frames. They are firm and keep the transparency from bending, and you can use the top of the frame for notes and numbering.

If you are using an overhead projector and screen, test it beforehand for focus, clarity, and brightness. When positioning the projector, remember that the closer the projector is to the screen, the smaller the image appears on the screen.

When it's time to show your transparency to the group, place it on the glass, *then* turn on the projector. Allow a moment before you speak — this gives the audience time to absorb the content. And remember that an empty white screen is hard on the eyes. If you are not ready to go to your next transparency immediately, cover the screen with a blank piece of paper or turn off the projector.

If your transparency has more than one point, cover the material that you are not discussing with a blank piece of paper, and reveal the material as you go from point to point.

As I've said before, always face your audience, not the screen. Also, do not feel you need to illustrate every point with a visual. Interaction with your audience is equally — if not more — important than your visuals.
It is a good idea to carry an extra bulb for your overhead projector. Bulbs can burn out at any time. Also, most overhead projectors are dusty and have fingerprints and lint on the lens. Dust it with a damp paper towel before your audience arrives.

New technology is continually becoming available to aid speakers and trainers. Although these new capabilities are powerful, it is easy to become *techostressed.* It takes time and energy to stay current with all the new options of presentation hardware and software, and it's easy to feel overwhelmed. But it's impossible to ignore the power and impact that the latest technological advances are bringing to speakers and trainers.

You can use presentation software to create your overheads and slide shows quickly and easily. Professional speakers and trainers now use Microsoft PowerPoint, a software program for designing visual aids. If you use a projector like the Proxima brand projector, your laptop computer can connect directly to the projector for a brilliant color presentation without the use of overheads. You can achieve animation and interesting "wipes" as one slide changes to the next. Sound can be added to animation, giving you a great deal of flexibility. In addition, PowerPoint checks your visuals for font size, grammar and spelling.

There are other ways that technology can come to the aid of speakers and trainers. Electronic whiteboards interface with computers and keep track of all text and print copies. This can certainly help eliminate excessive note taking. Panasonic offers a "Panaboard" that prints out multiple copies of everything you write on it, and it replaces the flip chart or an overhead projector and screen. It has an optional PC interface that enables you to fax, e-mail or add graphics. (See Resources page.)

Another advantage of electronic communication tools is that they allow you to edit at the last minute, while overhead transparencies and 35mm slides are not that flexible.

Many presenters use a relatively inexpensive, off-the-shelf presentation software package. PowerPoint, Presentations, Persuasion, Astound and Freelance Graphics all allow you to design slide shows, complete with sound and special effects including animation, graphs and charts. This gives you the ability to make presentations without special training and with minimal equipment.

Digital photography manipulates images and makes them sharper, clearer and faster. Document cameras can plug into video conferencing technology and transmit your presentation materials to monitors anywhere in the worl You can also use regular overhead transparencies with a document camera.

When swiveled sideways, document cameras can double as video-conferencing cameras. (Canon, Sony and Samsung make Document Cameras). They are sturdy, dependable and flexible enough to work with the presentation equipment that you already have. Document cameras can be found in many corporate boardrooms and conference facilities. They are commonly used in training, education and legal settings.

With this type of projector, you can also connect a VCR and project a television image onto the screen. While these projectors are expensive to own, they can be rented. Other computer software packages that you should consider include Harvard Graphics and Aldus Persuasion.

Computer-generated visuals have almost completely replaced traditional slides, overheads and transparencies. But these tried-and-true methods still have their champions. Although slides lack animation and special effects, they are convenient and reliable, and 35mm slides offer high resolution and sharp bright colors. (But for large groups, an LCD panel or projector is required.)

Be sure to place your slides in 80-slot carousels. The larger carousels have tighter slots, and I find the slides often jam. And a wireless remote allows you to face your audience and stand away from the projector while you advance your slides.

But be warned! Using 35mm slides and overhead slides gives a hidden message to your audience — you are in the Stone Age!

The World Wide Web and the corporate intranet are rapidly changing the very nature of meetings themselves. By using standard presentation software along with some add-on programs, you can convert existing presentations to be viewed at a meeting or downloaded from a Web page or corporate intranet.

Web conferencing is a new communications medium. It can be used in conjunction with teleconferencing. The teleconference delivers the audio and the web conference offers participants a way to see visual material and ask questions without interrupting the program.

Meetings are heading into cyberspace rapidly. Web-conferencing aims at small groups of up to 25 attendees and provides interactive application sharing, web touring and whiteboard annotation. Kept simple and short, Web-conferencing can be very effective in bringing people together when they are in different parts of the country and it saves a lot of travel expense and time. Web-casting can be used for large or small group meetings that require limited interaction, such as a keynote address. (See Resource page for Web-conference services.)

But don't think that technology is the only way to go. Props also provide wonderfully dramatic visual aids, and are often very simple objects. Ray Pelletier, CSP, (Certified Speaking Professional, a designation of superior platform skills from the National Speakers Association), was an outstanding coach and mentor. He would demonstrate fascinating magic tricks along with great motivation. Zig Ziglar uses a small water pump on stage to show you that you have to "prime the pump" for success. The great Ira Hayes handed out dollar bills to demonstrate his sales training message. A number of years ago, I gave a speech on "Tools For Success," and I actually placed a tool kit on the lectern, displaying many objects that would relate to my words.

Last, but not least, be sure to rehearse your presentation with your audiovisuals so they are in sync with your words. But a word of caution: Don't use visuals aids in place of a well prepared presentation. Do not rely on visuals to carry your speech. Oftentimes, less is more.

And remember, PowerPoint is a tool, not a crutch.

In review, it is a good idea to specifically request the equipment and room arrangement that you desire. Provide the meeting planner or program chairman with a written list of your needs.

AN EVENT CHECK LIST

Plan the room arrangement

The chairs

The podium

Placement of podium steps, height of podium

The lectern, placement and height

The location of lights, dimmer, spots, colored gels

Air conditioning controls

Sound system, microphone — attached to lectern, wireless, hand-held, lavaliere, clip-on

Tape recorder

Name and extension number of building engineer

Controls to close shades or curtains

Location of water and coffee

Overhead projector, extra bulbs, pointer, remote control

Transparencies, slides, film, videotape, 3/4" VHS, 1/2" VHS

Projection table

Screen placement, direction and visibility

Video monitors, placement and visibility

Flipchart easel, paper pads, Sanford color markers

Chalk board, chalk

Masking tape to attach flip chart papers to wall

Props

Extension cord

Duct tape to cover extension cords on the floor

Scotch or masking tape for door latch (stops the clicking sound when late comers arrive)

Name badges, name tents for tables

Ribbon to cordon back rows

Name of meeting planner or program chairman with phone numbers

Extra copy of your introduction and your notes

Controls to close intercom or piped in music

Evaluation sheets

Note pads, extra pencils

Front table for props, back table for product

Sign on the door with the name of the session

"Session in progress" sign

A sign requesting that all cell phones and beepers be turned off, no smoking sign

A note requesting that waiters refrain from serving/clearing during your presentation

Location of telephones, lavatories, fire exits

Business cards, cough drops, water, travel clock

Workbooks, reference materials, handout sheets

Token gifts for audience volunteers, the program chairman

QUICK REVIEW

THE ROOM ARRANGEMENT AFFECTS THE SPEAKER AND THE AUDIENCE

ARRIVE EARLY

CHECK THE ROOM ARRANGEMENT

THE CHAIRS

THE LIGHTING

THE ROOM TEMPERATURE

THE LECTERN

THE MICROPHONE

REHEARSE WITH YOUR A/V EQUIPMENT

CHECK OUT NEW TECHNOLOGY

> *PowerPoint*
> *Document cameras*
> *Electronic Whiteboards*
> *Web conferencing*
> *Web casting*

Part 4

IT'S TIME TO STAND AND DELIVER

"A glass of tea with a smiling face is better than a feast with a frown."

— Moroccan proverb

IT'S TIME TO STAND
AND DELIVER
YOUR NON-VERBAL MESSAGE

"The message and the messenger are a reflection of each other."
—*CKS*

<u>YOU ARE THE MESSAGE</u>

Your audience forms their opinion of you in the first thirty seconds of your speech, based on your image, educational level, friendliness, sincerity, social position, ethnic background and other factors. Most importantly, they decide whether they will stay tuned to your presentation.

It may seem that thirty seconds isn't long enough for them to get to know you. Actually, they made some of these judgements before you uttered your first words — as you walk to the podium, you are judged on your posture and carriage and the confidence you projected. It may not be fair, but every audience does it.

Roger Ailes, advisor to many United States presidents, top executives and author of *You Are The Message*, states, "Everything you do in relation to other people causes them to make judgements about what you stand for and what your message is."

You are the message! But are you sending a mixed message? Are you in synchronization with your words? Your body language, your eyes, your clothes, your posture, your voice — all these things add to your message. What does your image say about you? Does it say what you want it to say? Non-verbal communication extends to your smile, your posture, and how you do the simple things — wear your eyeglasses, handle your notes, stand at the lectern, and walk on and off the podium. In fact, your image begins when you arrive at the door, and it stays until you depart.

Because your image is so important, you want to portray a sense of confidence and control. When you are introduced, approach the podium with confident posture, a quick enthusiastic walk with shoulders relaxed. People believe that the way you hold yourself outwardly is the way you feel about yourself inwardly. Your face communicates your attitude, emotions, sincerity and enthusiasm.

Your audience will respond to your facial expression before they hear your words. My mother used to tell me " Don't frown, your face will freeze like that and when you get older, that is the way you will look" People do tell me that I smile a lot!
As the speaker, you are given the podium for the duration of your program. Consider it your space to control.

I have had clients say to me, "Carolyn, I just don't feel great confidence." I reply, "Confidence and high self-esteem are not things I can hand to you. But I can tell you what works — fake it till you make it!" If you *"do the action," the attitude will follow*

YOUR POSTURE

Start now. Walk straight and tall, as if you are royalty. Strong body language isn't just for your audience's benefit; it sends a message back to you. Good posture gives you confidence, power and energy. It's also good for your stomach muscles, diaphragm and spine.

When you arrive at the microphone, breathe, adjust the microphone, sweep the audience with your eyes, smile and begin.

Once you begin speaking, a little walking on the podium is acceptable. However, if your tendency is to march, rock back and forth, sway or two-step, you had better stay in one place... especially if the microphone is mounted on the lectern.

Watch those feet. You will look awkward if you tuck one foot behind the other ankle. On the other hand, don't stand stiff like a statue — that will keep you from appearing at ease and expressive

NERVOUS GESTURES

Nervous gestures are incomplete gestures with the arms and elbows pressed tightly against the body. Allow your gestures to be
open and broad. It may seem unnatural to you at first, possibly a bit too dramatic — but to your audience you will look confident and expressive.

When we feel tense, we tend to draw our shoulders upward toward our ears and hunch forward. That makes your breathing shallow, which in turn affects your speaking. So make an effort to relax your shoulders.

Some women have a tendency to tilt their head to one side after making a statement. It is a weak and indecisive gesture.

WHAT SHOULD I DO WITH MY HANDS?

I am always asked by my students, "What shall I do with my hands?" Here's what *not* to do: Don't lock them together. Don't hold hands with yourself. Don't hold your hands behind your back. What do you do? Just let them drop naturally at your side. And then when you say something expressive, allow your hands to extend that expressiveness.

Your hands and arms emphasize your words, so keep your hands out of your pockets. This is especially true if you have coins in your pockets. Better yet, remove the coins before you are introduced! Placing your hands together to form a steeple conveys confidence, but also smugness. It also can look like praying. Putting your hands on your hips looks aggressive and confrontational. Allow your arms to float freely at your side, your hands to reach out to the audience to emphasize your words.

Your non-verbal image includes the handling of notes at the lectern. As discussed in part three, notes should be inconspicuous, briefly glanced at and not be a distraction.

POINTLESS

But try not to point. I hate being in the audience when a speaker, trying to convey a message, jabs a finger toward the audience. It has a stabbing effect. The audience feels attacked, punished, or reprimanded.

People on TV are skilled at using gestures. As an experiment, mute the sound on your television and watch for non-verbal signals of actors and news anchors. You'll see that we generally use gestures in clusters. Notice which gestures are smooth and confident, and compare those to any gestures that may seem awkward.

This may seem like a lot of work, but the truth is — looking natural takes practice.

A CALL TO ARMS

In a conversation with one or two people, we generally keep our gestures above the waist and close to our bodies. But in front of an audience, small, close-to-your-body gestures look nervous and awkward. So when you're on-stage, make your gestures broad and expansive.

Be careful of postures that send the wrong message, such as folded arms (stern father), prayer gesture (sisters of mercy), the fig leaf lock (what are you hiding?), the arm flap (looks like an airplane), or hands clasped behind your back (referred to as handcuffed, hostage or parade rest). On the other hand, you distract your audience if you play with a pen, glasses, a book, your notes, or a pointer. And if you are standing next to the lectern, be careful not to use it as a crutch, leaning against it or draping yourself over it. .

When you motion to your audience with your arm reaching out, be sure your palm is facing up, a gesture perceived as friendly and inviting. When your palm is down with your finger pointing at the audience, they may consider it rude and challenging.

Gestures don't have to be fleeting or momentary. Holding your gesture and your gaze for just a moment can add impact and emphasis to your words.

THE EYES HAVE IT

"The eyes have it" for sincerity, for inspiring trust, for bridging with your audience and for getting your message across. The eyes are a pathway to the soul and direct eye contact shouts confidence. When Senator Bob Dole was running for president, he blinked a lot when he was interviewed by the press. It gave the viewer an impression that he was nervous and insecure. Possibly he was wearing contact lenses or his eyes were dry, but the repeated blinking was a distraction.

If you do wear glasses, keep them on. Some speakers have a habit of removing them and then putting them back on every time they begin a new idea. Any repetitive action can easily become a distraction to your audience.

Speak and look at your audience, not at your visuals, a screen, the flipchart, your notes, the floor or the ceiling. I once went to a lecture where the presenter kept her eyes on the wall over the heads of her audience throughout the whole presentation. Later, she told me she had memorized her speech and was visualizing it written on the back wall. It's an interesting technique, but as you can imagine, she was not effective. People in the audience kept looking over their shoulders trying to figure out what she was staring at.

And don't stare at the floor. It implies a lack of confidence, and no one buys from downcast eyes. You want to maintain eye contact with your audience. Keep a small travel clock or watch near your notes so that you can glance at the time without the audience being aware of it. If you have a large audience, direct your eye contact to all the corners and the center of the room. This makes everyone feel included and personally addressed.

If you walk into the audience, don't stay there very long — the front part of the audience has to turn and strain to hear and see you. On the other hand, if you stand off to one side for very long, part of your audience will leave with a stiff neck. Keep *all* areas of your audience in mind.

A few years ago, I received notice of a program being presented by a well known professor and authority on the art of the primitive tribes of Papua, New Guinea. Even though the museum was a 45 minute drive, I had recently returned from New Guinea and I knew this would be an interesting evening.

When I arrived, the museum was crowded with an expectant audience. When the speaker was introduced, he walked to the podium, placed his notes on the lectern... and proceeded to read his speech in a dull monotone, not even once looking up to make eye contact with his audience.

You would think that a renowned authority on a subject could relate interesting information and stories without reading from a text, wouldn't you? Or at least display some level of enthusiasm? Later, driving home, I thought, "Next time, just fax me the speech and I'll read it in the comfort of my office."

THINGS YOU SHOULD NEVER DO

When you're in front of an audience, here's a list of things you should NEVER do: chew gum, play with your cuff links or jewelry, jiggle coins in your pocket, twist your hair, or wear your hair so that it covers your eyes. Don't stroke your beard, crack your knuckles, or pick your nails. And above all, wherever it itches, don't scratch.

Finally, good posture costs nothing and pays a lot. You can start right now to be aware of how you stand and walk. Recording yourself on video is an excellent way to see yourself as others see you. You may be surprised at how you project yourself, and you will notice habits that you were not previously aware of.

YOUR TURN AT THE LECTERN

Now, you are ready to step up to the lectern, put your notes down, adjust the microphone, sweep the audience with your eyes, breathe, smile and begin. Unfortunately, when some people arrive at the lectern they turn a bright pink.

Blushing, a non -verbal response that happens to many people, is not something we can control, but there are some things you can do to help. I suggest that you avoid caffeine — whether in coffee, tea or chocolate — prior to speaking, and stay away from alcohol or spicy foods.

If you blush anyway, be aware that your audience won't notice it. Just forget it! Besides, having extra color in your face makes you look healthy. As you become more comfortable on the platform, your tendency to blush will vanish.

CLOTHES COMMUNICATE
TAKE AN IMAGE INVENTORY

Your clothes communicate to your audience before you utter your first word. Clothes project an attitude, and what you wear gives your audience a message, loud and clear.

Your appearance also offers clues as to how you see yourself. Are you wrinkled, disheveled, colorless, flashy, overdressed, or gaudy? If so, these images immediately take credibility away from your message. The bottom line is, if your clothes are inappropriate, it can distract from your message.

Your attire should be professional Be as well dressed as your audience. For men, the conservative business suit is most desirable. If the occasion is an informal business meeting at a resort, you may consider slacks and a sport jacket. A jacket maintains the decorum of the professional presenter, and it is always a sign of authority. When you are standing, a jacket looks best buttoned; however, when you sit, unbutton the jacket so it doesn't pull around the buttons. Remove bulky wallets, coins, and handkerchief from your pockets beforehand.

For women, a linen or wool pants outfit is in good taste. I sometimes present in dresses, but they are always very tailored and have long sleeves. For shoes, a closed pump is more professional in appearance than open-toed sandals. Save the splashy floral prints for garden parties and revealing blouses for the cocktail parties.

Take care with accessories. Too much jewelry or anything that clangs, flashes or swings can distract your audience. Miniskirts can be a problem if you are on a high platform stage. Finally, your audience will notice if your shoes are scruffy, so keep them clean and shined. Shoes should be the same color or darker than your pants or skirt.

Why should you be so concerned with your appearance? After all, isn't it your message that's important? Remember that your audience's belief system says, "You get what you see." And your audience members will be asking, "Why should I believe this speaker?"

I've learned a lot of this the hard way. One afternoon, I was speaking to an association in Orlando. I wore a lovely beige suit with a cream blouse. I thought I looked quite elegant, but after the presentation someone came up to me and commented that it was difficult to see me.

Was I invisible? It turned out that the wall behind me was beige, my suit was beige, and my hair is blond. I must have faded into the background! Since that occasion, I always include some color in my outfit. If I wear a navy suit, I wear a red blouse. And I have a collection of scarves that can add some zip to any of my suits.

But color can work to your disadvantage too. One day I presented a full day workshop in a fire engine red suit. At the end of the day, a participant came up to me and said, "I love red, but watching you all day in that bright red suit has caused eye strain." Oh well, live and learn.

As my red suit proved, color affects your audience. With this in mind, give some advance thought to your presentation outfit. Avoid a busy pattern; it can make your audience dizzy. Forget floral patterns; it will look like you are going to a garden party. Forget miniskirts; they can be a problem when you're on a high stage. And revealing blouses are definitely a distraction. Clothes cover over sixty-five percent of your body, so it is important to "dress to impress and to dress to express." The way you dress will express your authenticity, professionalism and authority.

Men look excellent in navy and dark gray suits with narrow pinstripes and a conservative, simple patterned tie. (A man's tie is his signature). Black, navy and dark gray are authoritative colors. An all-black suit, however, can be overpowering, intimidating, and funeral-like.

Men's clothes should be of good fabric and well- tailored. A tie that is too long or too short is a distraction so the tip of a man's tie should hit the middle of his belt buckle. Ties range from conservative to good taste to garish. They are visible and the make a statement. Heed on the side of conservative. Make sure that your outfit is not dated.

Clothing styles, make-up, and hairstyles should always be current. I hope that you are not wearing the same hairstyle you wore in college.

Is your visual message as strong as your speech? If you look coordinated, bright, and up-to-date, people will believe your material is current, bright and coordinated. Clothes and make-up should never distract from the message.

One last thought — it's a good idea to keep a list of what you wear to each engagement so you don't repeat the same outfit to the same audience if you're invited back.

SPEAKING WITH STYLE

"The single greatest secret for giving a great speech or presentation can be summed up in one word — passion. If you've got passion you can break every rule of presenting and you will still succeed."
— *Bryan Mattimore, author of 99% Inspiration.*

When a speaker draws your attention, holds your attention, and has a message you can understand, that speaker has style. If a speaker presents ideas that penetrate your mind, linger in your thoughts, or touch your emotions, that speaker has style. Style is defined in your gestures, voice, emotion, sincerity and words.

If presenters sound as if they are on autopilot or bored with their own material, or if their speeches are canned or patched together without structure, their presentations will certainly be lacking in style.

Style is your audience's perception of you. Style captivates your audience. Your audience wants to know how much you care before they care how much you know.

It is interesting to observe some well known speakers and the styles they display. General Norman Schwarzkopf has a style that comes across as "being in charge," direct and competent. Les Brown, CPAE, and Tony Robbins move their audiences with a rapid, motivational delivery and a message that conveys, "I can achieve, and so can you!" Zig Ziglar, CPAE, offers homespun, humorous, spiritual, and highly motivating speeches laced with practical "how to" insights. Paul Harvey has a recognizable style with melodramatic inflection, extremely long pauses, and staccato sentences.

Franklin D. Roosevelt and Walter Cronkite both portrayed the style of caring grandfathers. Their manner of speaking made their audiences feel secure and safe during tumultuous times. Winston Churchill appeared spontaneous, even though he spent hours in preparation. He also wore his glasses on the tip of his nose, which gave him the appearance of looking directly at his audience when in reality he read from his notes.

John F. Kennedy, with his strong New England accent and fast pace, never left the lectern. His style of passion and conviction was made memorable by his use of easily remembered, repetitive phrases. Ted Sorensen, Special Counsel and speech writer to John F. Kennedy, studied Lincoln's Gettysburg Address before drafting Kennedy's inaugural address. Sorensen realized that Lincoln never used a two or three syllable word where one syllable would do, and he never used two or three words when one would be sufficient.

Without a doubt, the prize for the most style goes to Elizabeth Dole. Her walk among the audience, Oprah style, at the 1996 Republican convention in San Diego was wonderful. She was the first to bring the talk-show format to the floor of a national political convention. Her break with tradition charmed her audience.

Elizabeth Dole did not use notes, Teleprompter or cue-cards. At the beginning, her lapel microphone buzzed and fizzled, so without hesitation she switched to a handheld microphone (a good example of preplanning preparation by having a back-up). Her opening remarks were "I am going to be speaking with friends, and I'm going to be speaking about the man I love." As she roamed through the crowd, Elizabeth's great personal charisma and warmth came across to her audience. ABC's Peter Jennings said "It was an impressive piece of stagecraft. She electrified the crowd."

President George Bush often speaks in a mixed, somewhat abbreviated syntax. In his State of the Union message, he asked, "Ambitious aims? Of course! Easy to do? Far from it!" This truncated syntax style was tagged "Bush Talk," short staccato sentences that don't always connect. As former President Bush has said, "They're doing that story thing. Claim I talk funny. Worried? Not at this juncture. Wouldn't be prudent. Still president.

Sometimes he would get lost before he got to the point. His style, at times referred to as the "me-Tarzan-you-Jane oratory," was unorthodox. Despite this, he was still able to portray sincerity and conviction.

But even an experienced speaker like Bush can make mistakes. Once he glanced at his watch during a televised debate with Bill Clinton in 1992. The audience wondered, did he have to be someplace else, or did he want the debate to end? Checking his watch while he was onstage made the audience uncomfortable.

His son, George W. has a much more effective speaking style. After winning a second term in office, his demeanor became more confident. Granted, he has been known to make some confusing statements such as: "The vast majority of our imports come from outside the country," "If we don't succeed, we run the risk of failure," "The future will be better tomorrow," and "A low voter turnout is an indication of fewer people going to the polls." Despite this, George W. had no problem being more animated and effective on the platform than Al Gore, who was variously described as wood, cardboard and granite. Gore would flood his speeches with too much information, and at the same time seemed to talk down to the audience as if they were in elementary school.

Barbara Bush is a natural, warm and credible speaker. Ronald Reagan had charisma and warmth and it came through in his speeches. He sounded like a good actor portraying the president. Harry Truman was not a great speaker, but his style came across as direct, straight talk — let's get to the bottom line and get results.

Winston Spencer Churchill is widely regarded as one of the best speakers of our time. On October 29, 1941, Churchill addressed the Harrow Boys School. This was his never-to-be-forgotten speech. "Never give in. Never, never, never, never give in. In anything great or small, large or petty — never give in except to convictions of honor and good sense." Then he sat down. That was his entire speech. A great example that you can be brief and powerful at the same time.

Peggy Noonan, special assistant to President Reagan, a presidential speech writer and the author of *Simply Speaking*, wrote George Bush's "Thousand Points of Light" and "Read My Lips" speeches. Peggy says speeches have defined and shaped American history, from Lincoln's "Gettysburg Address" to Martin Luther King Jr.'s 1963 "I have A Dream" and JFK's 1961 Inaugural Address in which he said, "Ask not what your country can do for you; ask what you can do for your country." Pulitzer Prize author and poet Carl Sandberg described Kennedy's address was Lincolnesque.

Robert Dole, the 1996 republican candidate for president, could not project on television. He has a flat midwestern voice with very little inflection, mostly a monotone, constant blinking and not too much smiling. He does not bring any emotion into his voice so there is no emphasis on his important points. To put it bluntly, his delivery is wooden. In person, one on one, he has great wit, but it did not show on the podium. He was used to speaking on the Senate floor, but that style is not effective on television. Dole has always referred to himself as "a doer, not a talker." It possibly cost him the election.

It was August 23, 1963 and Martin Luther King Jr. had written his speech the evening before. It was a good speech — politically sound and motivational, but certainly not historic. Masses of people gathered at the Lincoln Memorial. Two hours before the rally was to begin, the crowd swelled to between 200,000 and 300,000 people. The program of speakers and singers went on for three hours. Fatigue was setting in. Mahalia Jackson sang a spiritual that brought tears to people's eyes. The crowd was restless and trying to avoid sunstroke in the August heat.

King was introduced. He began his prepared speech — but part way through it, he stopped. He abandoned his prepared script and extemporaneously began, "I have a dream…." Enveloping "My country 'tis of thee," "… from every mountainside let freedom ring!" and ending with an old spiritual, "Free at last, free at last! Thank God Almighty, we are free at last," King set aside his lofty canned words and replaced them with passion. The timbre of his voice and the power coming straight from his heart rocked the crowd. His words, never to be forgotten, pulsated over the throngs and throughout the nation, remains one of the greatest speeches along with Lincoln, Churchill and Kennedy.

Bill Clinton is a polished speaker with good pacing and perfect pauses; he uses humor and has a "bring it down to the basics" manner of explaining complex issues. He is an expert at fielding questions. Even though his voice is chronically hoarse, no one connects better with an audience than Bill Clinton. His style is eager intensity sprinkled with humor.

Mother Theresa read all of her speeches in a singsong monotone, rarely looking up from her notes. Despite this, she was overwhelmingly effective. (Every rule has a rare exception.)

Colin Powell has great platform charisma, and audiences respond to his self-deprecating humor balanced with his strength and authenticity.

Richard Nixon arrived for the first televised presidential debate pale, sweating profusely, and in pain from an injured knee. He refused any make-up and he leaned to the side of the lectern. Kennedy, tanned, confident, and relaxed with erect posture and television makeup won the debate… and the election.

Bill Gove, CSP (certified speaking professional) and CPAE, was the first President of the National Speakers Association. A world-class speaker, he was honored with Toastmasters International's highest award, The Golden Gavel. Bill had a wonderful conversational quality when he spoke, with great pauses, gestures and humorous stories. It was a unique style that was all his own.

Style comes with being authentic and offering genuine self-expression. Audiences today are jaded; they have heard it all before. They have little patience for phony motivation, platitudes, pretension, and time-worn cliches. But if you are authentic and sincere, your audience will believe that you "walk your talk."

Mae West, a favorite philosopher of mine, once said, "It's not what you say, it's how you say it. It's not what you do, it's how you do it — and how you look when you say it and do it!"

Isn't that what I have said throughout this book?

As you accept more and more speaking opportunities and your confidence level improves, your own style will emerge. Your style will come with your sincerity, enthusiasm for your topic, and interest in your audience. Style comes with thorough knowledge of your topic.

DEFINING YOUR STYLE

As you can see from the following examples, your personality affects your delivery style. Regardless of profession or walk of life, there are four basic personality styles. You are probably a blend of more than one style, but basically you react and perform most frequently in just one style. Where do you see yourself? And how can you improve?

The Dominant Director

This is a bottom-line person, a decision maker who likes to be in control. This person is direct and results-oriented, and speaks fast and to the point. A Dominant Director delivers speeches that are specific, clear and decisive, with strong conclusions. They tell their audience just what results they want... and they expect them to comply.

To be more effective: A Dominant Director should speak slower, allow time for questions, be patient, listen to the audience, and try to sound less demanding.

The Enthusiastic Energizer

Here is someone who is likes to be around people. Enthusiastic Energizers enjoy speaking to an audience. Their speeches are colorful and paint word pictures. They use humor enhanced with lively stories. Their speeches are creative but often lack structure. Because they always make use of humor, their audiences enjoy their performances.

To be more effective: The EnthusiasticEnergizer should be careful to include accurate details, back-up information with solid facts, and keep on track.

The Reliable Responsive

This speaker is audience centered and audience-involved. Often motivational, Reliable Responsives offer explanations to be sure that the audience understands their message. They build bridges with the audience. Their speeches are well structured and have a conversational quality. The audience can easily relate to this speaker's style. The Reliable Responsive is responsive to the audiences' needs.

To be more effective: The Reliable Responsive should try to be more flexible and creative, add humor, and expand on storytelling.

The Analytical Analyzer

The Analytical Analyzer is detail-oriented and always well prepared. This speaker makes strong use of facts, graphs, logic, and rational points. Their speeches are orderly and offer great attention to detail; however, their audiences must stay alert to digest all the facts thrown at them.

To be more effective: The Analytical Analyzer should avoid relying on an overdose of charts and graphs, and should not rely on too much material to get to the basics. He should also incorporate story telling and word pictures, show enthusiasm, and smile more.

Your audience is also made up of all of these personality styles.
You can identify some common characteristics of these styles. Remember, many people are a blend of more than one style. Craft your presentation style to reach out to their different needs.

THE AUDIENCE

The Dominant Director: They are decisive and results oriented. They want the speaker to get to the point. Bring up facts not feelings. Don't bore them with details. They want to know the bottom line and make their own decisions. The speaker better end on time or they become impatient. Their questions will be direct and they expect direct answers.

The Enthusiastic Energizer: Is friendly, open to audience involvement, thinks role playing and inter-active workshops are great. They hope that the presenter is entertaining, will use colorful visuals and does not go into too much detail or be too technical.

They usually are the first ones to participate and ask questions.

Reliable Responsive: These are the team players They like the speaker to be organized and follow an agenda. They look for sincerity and optimism. Their concerns are: How will the speakers' ideas effect change. They are good listeners and will give the speaker a chance before judging.

The Analytical Analyzer: They like facts, details, statistics and information provided on grafts and charts. Does the speaker have data to back up these statements. They want proof of the information presented. They often feel that the speaker is speaking too fast because they want to write notes on everything said.
They don't enjoy audience inter-action but they do like to be given projects and challenges as long as you can give them adequate time to do it thoroughly.

QUICK REVIEW

YOUR ARE THE MESSAGE

DOES YOUR BODY LANGUAGE SYNCHRONIZE WITH YOUR WORDS

YOUR HANDS AND ARMS SHOULD EMPHASIZE YOUR WORDS

EYE CONTACT RELATES SINCERITY AND BONDS WITH THE AUDIENCE

GOOD POSTURE DOESN'T COST ANYTHING, BUT PAYS A LOT

THE AUDIENCE BELIEVES "WHAT YOU SEE IS WHAT YOU GET"

CLOTHES COMMUNICATE A MESSAGE, - IS IT PROFESSIONAL, SUCCESSFUL, CREDIBLE

SPEAK WITH STYLE

DEFINE YOUR STYLE

DOMINANT DIRECTOR

ENTHUSIASTIC ENERGIZER

RELIABLE RESPONSIVE

ANALYTICAL ANALYZER

THE STYLE OF THE AUDIENCE

Part 5

WORD POWER

"Half the world is composed of people who have something to say and can't, the other half has nothing to say and they keep saying it."

— Robert Frost

THE POWER OF YOUR WORDS

THE PAUSE THAT REFRESHES

Your voice can support you or it can sabotage you. It is a clue to your personality. Overusing the expressions "You know," "You know what I mean?" or "You know what I'm talking about?" shows an inability to verbalize your thoughts. Likewise, using *um*, *ah*, *er*, or *OK* as fillers detracts from your message and its effectiveness.

Powerful speaking means avoiding clichés, those overused trite expressions like, "Unaccustomed as I am to public speaking…," "Without further ado…," "Last but not least…," "He needs no introduction…," and "First and foremost…." If you normally employ these phrases, then stop now. They are the junk food of language. As soon as you learn to replace these fillers with pauses, you will elevate your speaking skills dramatically.

All of these habits result from a fear of dead air, or speaking ahead of yourself. It's fairly easy to rid yourself of these unnecessary "fillers." Just practice replacing them with simple pauses. It can feel awkward at first, but the results will astound you.

THE PAUSE IS SPEAKING PUNCTUATION

The pause is a form of "speaking punctuation" similar to using a comma or period when writing. A pause in a speech gives your audience an opportunity to digest what you just said. (This is especially important if you talk fast or if you're throwing a lot of content at the audience.) The pause is like a rest stop on a long trip. It's refreshing.

Pauses are powerful, and you should definitely use pauses more effectively in your speaking style. Add pauses for drama, emphasis and effect. The pause creates suspense, it packs power, it brings your audience to attention, and it creates tension. A pause can set a mood and add dimension to your speech. A pause creates anticipation. (Think of Beethoven's Fifth Symphony without pauses. It wouldn't be the same, would it?)

Many people are uncomfortable with pauses because it seems they last so lo-o-o-ong. Remember, a pause doesn't seem nearly as long to your audience as it does to you. Pauses can range from two to 10 seconds — or more.

If you incorporate humor into your speech (and you should), the pause is essential for a number of reasons. It gives the audience a chance to "catch on" to your humor. And you certainly do not want to speak on top of their laughter; they won't hear what you're saying. So pausing after a humorous remark is a necessity.

Jack Benny, the famous comedian, was famous for his pauses. He said, "Timing is not so much knowing when to speak, but knowing when to pause."

There are many different types of pauses —

The pause after you have been introduced and you have thanked the introducer (and before you actually start your speech.)It gets your audience's attention. It is much more effective than talking the moment you arrive at the lectern.

The reflective pause is used after you have said something significant. It gives your audience a chance to write it down.

The dramatic pause is used to create anticipation.

The "I'm thinking" pause looks like you're hunting for the right word. You appear spontaneous and not "canned."

The control pause regains control of the audience. Heads will rise as they return their attention to you. This is also effective when there are separate conversations going on or you have people distracting the group. Just stop and look in that direction.

The "any questions?" pause gives your audience a chance to think.

The waiting for a reaction pause. A chance to receive laughter after you have said something humorous. Or made A statement that will elicit applause. But don't pause too long in case the laughter and applause doesn't come

A transitional pause separates your ideas or begins a new portion of your talk.

Your audience goes into "inner dialog" when you pause. It gives them time to think, digest and absorb. A brief two-second pause at the close of your speech is very effective. Rather than sprinting to your seat as if you are glad it is over, or offering a thank you at the end of your last sentence — just pause. This allows the audience to show their appreciation and allows you the moment to accept their applause.

The power of pauses is widely recognized. Many years ago, the Coca Cola company used "The pause that refreshes" as an advertisement. And Mark Twain described the pause most effectively when he said, "A pause is that impressive silence, that eloquent silence, that geometrically progressive silence which often achieves a desired effect where no combination of words, however felicitous, could accomplish the same effect."

<u>YOUR TONE, PITCH AND VOLUME SPEAK FOR YOU</u>

How you say what you say tells your audience a lot about you, so be careful of the tone of your voice. Speaking too loud sounds crude. A harsh voice makes you sound "tough" like a gangster, while a soft voice sounds childlike and timid. If you speak too quickly, you sound insincere. Also, your audience can't keep up with you. They get tired and give up trying to listen. If you speak too slowly, you sound depressed, boring, tiring and unenthusiastic. Your audience will become impatient and they'll lose interest and daydream.

Because your skull interferes with your hearing, it is very hard to hear your own voice accurately. So tape your speeches so you can listen to yourself, or ask for feedback from a trusted friend or associate. Have them tell you if you speak too quickly, too slowly, or in a monotone.

Some celebrities have very distinct, recognizable voices: Melanie Griffith's childlike whisper, Jackie Kennedy's breathy patrician whisper, Kathleen Turner's sexy smoky deep voice, Lauren Bacall's upper-class cat food commercials, Julia Child's squeaky chalk-on-a-blackboard, Candice Bergen's wise guy contralto.

What about today's stars? Sly Stallone's mumbling Bronx, Rosanne Barr's streetwise, Fran Drescher's high Brooklynese, and Woody Allen's whiney New York. Sadly, television talk has taken us to a new low. Many popular screen stars today, such as Tom Cruise, Harrison Ford and Kevin Costner, have flat ordinary voices (although that has not seemed to hurt them at the box office).

A high pitched voice is difficult to listen to and lacks power and authority whereas speaking at a lower pitch sounds more commanding and in-control. This gives men an advantage, but women who are able to lower the pitch of their voice can also sound more authoritative.

Try this simple exercise to deepen your voice. Sit on a chair, bend over, and drop your head to your knees. Now start talking. Do you hear how your voice level descends? You can also maintain that lower pitch with your head upright.

Finally, if you end your sentences on a high vocal note, your statements will sound more like questions and they'll lose their impact. Audio tape yourself and decide if this is something you need to work on.

MONOTOUS MONOTONE

How's your vocal variety? A monotone voice is like a face without a smile. A voice with no expression is bland and uninteresting.

Can you image listening to a symphony that had only one tone, and no variety to the music? Vocal variety and inflections create flavor and add emotion to your message. To avoid speaking in a monotone, vary your pitch, tone and volume. Emphasize words, and use pauses appropriately.

Changing the inflection of just one word in a sentence can give it a completely different meaning. Consider this sentence: "Today is your birthday." Now say it four times, putting emphasis on a different word each time:

> *Today is your birthday. (This is the date of your birthday.)*
> *Today is your birthday. (Today really is your birthday.)*
> *Today is your birthday. (It's not my birthday; it's yours.)*
> *Today is your birthday. (It's a special day.)*

Varying the emphasis on a single word changes the meaning of the entire sentence. This shows the advantage that speech has over text.

Don't make the listener work hard to hear your words. Speak up and speak out! Use variety and pacing. It's the only way to get your message across.

Mumblers can be better understood if they open their jaws and project. Nasality is often caused by not opening the jaws wide enough while speaking.
Breathlessness can be corrected by taking slower and deeper breaths.

Practice projecting your voice by bringing it from your diaphragm and directing it to the back of the room. Think you're too loud? Remember that you usually sound louder to yourself than you do to the audience. Consequently, most beginning speakers hold back and do not utilize the strength of their voices. They under-emphasize, under-project, and inhibit their range.

There are three types of vocal variety. 1. Loud almost a shout and soft like a whisper. 2. Saying a word very slowly emphasizing each syllable.

Example; The dinner was won-der-ful. 3. Using a pause before and after a word. Example; We drove down a—-dangerous—-road.

Your entire audience needs to hear you, so focus on making your voice reach the last row. And when you raise your volume, you get another benefit — your energy level increases.

CONVERSATIONAL LANGUAGE

Use conversational language when you speak. Make the words your own, reflecting your personality. Avoid "techno speak" and "hyper babble" such as, "Pulchritude possesses solely coetaneous profundity." (It means: beauty is only skin deep.) Do you know that "acerb clusters of viniferous spheroids" is just a fancy way of saying "sour grapes"? And don't inundate your audience with excessive information. If you give people too many facts and figures, they "close their ears." Most audiences are technophobic; they depend on you to simplify ideas and theories.

By all means, avoid profanity. And don't try to sound "with it" by using contemporary colloquialisms, especially if they are in questionable taste. Compare your voice, tone and pronunciation with that of network news commentators. Use positive statements and leave out qualifiers such as, "I hope," "I think," "sort of," "kind of," and "I guess." Instead, make concrete, direct statements.

Once in a while, a speaker will begin with an apology. Don't apologize for your lack of experience, lack of preparation, being nervous, or your topic. Your audience will feel like they are getting second best. It's a downer right at the beginning.

If your throat feels dry before speaking, suck on a cough drop or drink tepid water or tea. Never drink cold liquids prior to speaking, because it constricts the throat muscles. Also, avoid milk and other dairy products prior to speaking. Dairy products cause phlegm to form in your throat. And don't indulge in a heavy meal just before a presentation; it zaps your energy.

Keep a watch or clock within your view while you're speaking, so you don't have to guess how much time you've got left. As the speaker, it is your obligation to end on time, as much as you would like to include all of your material. Audiences resent speakers who go over the time limit, even if they started late because of activities preceding them.

REGIONAL DIALECTS

Speakers who feel their regional dialect or foreign accent interferes with their message can contact David Alan Stern, PhD, of Dialect Accent Specialists Inc. (See Resources page.) He can supply information to help your presentation voice.

Dr. Morton Cooper, author of *Change Your Voice, Change Your Life*, has made great strides with high-pitched and strangled-sounding voices as well as many other disorders.

Finally, the American Management Association offers an audio cassette, *American Accent Program*. (See Resources)

Common Words Often Mispronounced

Word	Mispronounced
schedule	sched-al
hundred	hunderd
secretary	sec-a-tary
especially	ex-pecially
picture	pitcher
anyway	anyways

Word	**Mispronounced**
regular	regalur
battery	battree
suppose	spose
supposed to	spos to
Washington	Warshington
scared	a-scared
restaurant	restrunt
frustrated	fustrated
similar	simlar
accurate	accret
manufacture	mana-facture
figure	figgur
problem	probum
usually	usally
recurring	re-accuring
Tuesday	toosday
length	lenth
library	Liberry

Word	Mispronounced
probably	problee
Athlete	athalete
Ask	aks
Idea	idear
Going to	gonna
Want to	wanna
Because	cuz
Theatre	the-a-ter
You	yous
Was	wus
I said	I says
Nuclear	nuc-you-ler
Realtor	real-a-tor

INTERACT WITH YOUR AUDIENCE, INVOLVE THEIR PARTICIPATION

"A speech is a two-way conversation. Even if the audience doesn't say a word, they react."

— Unknown

I am standing in the meeting room. As often happens, the audience is slow in arriving. Most of the people sit in the middle of the room or further back. I walk around and introduce myself.

But I'm also doing something else — I'm selecting volunteers to participate in my program. I'm giving them prewritten questions for the Q&A portion of the presentation. Although some are pleased to participate, others are reluctant and fear being called upon, they resist interaction during a workshop.

Yet all of my workshops are interactive. Why? Because being involved in the program is the best way to learn and retain new information. I don't engage my audience in endless games. But I always find a way to involve my audience with the information that I am presenting

<u>BRING YOUR AUDIENCE INTO YOUR SPEECH</u>

Audience participation connects your audience to your program. It allows them not only to hear and see your message, but to experience it. Although audience participation can occur spontaneously, the best thing to do is to plan your audience participation when you're developing your presentation.

Because it can be uncomfortable to ask for volunteers during the presentation and have no one volunteer, I find my volunteers *before* the presentation begins. I only select those who are receptive to participating. If an audience member is reluctant, I don't coax. They may be painfully shy, or there can be many other reasons why they may not wish to participate. If a person declines, I respect their wishes.

Luckily, there are usually some extroverts who enjoy being in the spotlight.

I use all sorts of interactive activities. Most audiences enjoy role-playing exercises. In case they're unfamiliar with the role-playing exercise that you want, offer them examples of what they're to do before they begin. Then, be sure to thank each volunteer and ask the audience to show their appreciation with applause. I often give the participants a small token gift as I escort them off the platform.

When I conduct a workshop with a relatively small number of participants, I begin with a blank flipchart and I ask the group to tell me why they chose to attend my session. Questions I ask include: What information did they anticipate receiving? What are their particular concerns about the topic to be presented? In other words, "What brings you out of your office and away from customers to sit in this room — other than the great coffee?" Their responses help me to focus on the information I plan to present. Participants appreciate having a voice in the material that will be presented to them. But I'm doing something else as well — I am involving the audience immediately.

I find it effective to provide cardboard name cards in front of each participant (if the room is set up in classroom style), with their first names facing me so that I may call them by their names rather than pointing. This helps get my interactive activities going.

When I conduct a workshop, I pause part way through and ask the audience to take a minute and write down any "action ideas" or
new thoughts that have been stimulated by the workshop.

Asking questions opens audience participation — especially "open ended" questions (also called "toss up" questions). But be prepared to answer the question if no one responds. And extra care has to be taken with the "direct question" that is aimed at one person in the audience. Be sure to mention that person's name *before* asking the question, just in case that person isn't paying attention. In that case, they'll probably ask you to repeat the question, which is embarrassing for both of you.

THE APATHETIC AUDIENCE

The apathetic audience is one that was forced to be there. Many times they are indifferent and they don't want to be involved. In such a situation, don't start with interactive activities too soon. Rather than ask them why they're at the session (you won't like their answers), just give them a list of the benefits they will derive from your presentation.

In that case, a good interactive exercise to start with would be for the participants to have a few moments to share ideas on the topic with the person next to them. It will warm up the room and get them to express themselves, but not give anyone the opportunity to air their grievances in public.

During the breaks I suggest exercises and mini-assignments that encourage mingling and discussion while they're enjoying their coffee.

Whatever interactive activities you choose, remember that there is a difference between employing audience interaction and having the audience believe it is of value to them. You need to define the value to them before they'll "buy into" your activities.

SUGGESTIONS FOR GROUP INTERACTION

An ice breaker is a ship that cuts a path through frozen waters. In a meeting, an icebreaker clears the path for interaction and communication between the participants. Forcing individuals to interact, which can meet with resistance, you should tell participants why you are putting them through the exercise. Icebreakers can be used anytime, not just to open a meeting. An icebreaker triggers enthusiasm and involvement. An excellent resource for icebreakers and audience interaction is *Games Trainers Play* by Robert Pike. (See Resources page)

If your audience is small, begin with self-introductions. Audience involvement can be arranged even if you are addressing a large audience in an auditorium. You can ask people to share an idea with the person in the next seat. You can have your audience sitting at round tables, with each table holding a discussion on a different topic. The members at each table can be offered a choice of topics, or they can change tables every 1/2 hour to pick a different topic. Again, this is where name tents are very handy.

ICE BREAKERS

When I break the audience into groups, either I assign a leader for each group, or I have them choose their own leaders. I instruct the leaders to make sure everyone in their group has the opportunity to express his or her ideas. After they have had their discussion, the appointed leaders share their discussion ideas with the entire audience. Leaders can be chosen by their birthdays, who has the longest name, or simply by volunteering. Breaking the audience into groups works very well, especially in Mind Mapping exercises and problem solving.

Note: breakout groups usually result in a lot of conversation and noise within the room. When I want them to return their attention to me, I've found that ringing a small but loud bell is quite effective.

Another method that I use to involve my audience is to prepare 3x5 cards with prewritten questions and plant them in the audience. Some of the questions are intentionally funny, and this generates laughter, which invites further discussion.

Whatever interactive activities you choose, you'll discover that audience involvement brings home the information you are offering. When the audience participates in the process, they learn and experience at the same time.

ANSWERING CHALLENGING QUESTIONS
WHILE KEEPING COOL, CREDIBLE AND IN CONTROL

When you have finished your speech, you may believe the hard part is over. Watch out! If you are not careful, your credibility can diminish during the question-and-answer part of your presentation, and you will see your excellent closing remarks dissolve.

The question and answer segment is also part of your speech and must be considered during your preparation time. The Q&A session is important — sometimes it is the only opportunity that the audience has to participate in an exchange of information. It also gives you an opportunity to re-emphasize important points and add additional material.

Your Q&A session will be easier for you if you consider the following points. The main thing is to stay centered, in control of the audience, and be confident because you have prepared for this session.

Each question actually has three parts —
> 1) The question itself
> 2) Your answer
> 3) The bridge connecting it to your agenda

Here's an example:
(audience question) Has there been noticeable pollution from your factory?
(your answer) Yes, there was a measurable amount…
(bridge to topic) That is why last year we installed all new equipment, and set up new measuring standards that are in place right now.

Here are some important guidelines for handling questions from your audience:

Repeat the question. This serves two purposes — it allows the entire audience to hear the question, and it gives you a moment to think about your answer.

Treat all questions with respect. Never make anyone sorry they asked a question. Show your respect by offering direct eye contact to the person asking the question.

Keep your responses brief. Don't turn your answer into another speech.

When you select a member of your audience to ask a question and you don't know the person's name, gesture at them with your palm upward. Pointing at them with your palm down is threatening and possibly offensive.

Sometimes you have the option of handing out blank 3x5 cards in advance for your audience members to write their questions on, then gathering them during a break. This helps you select the questions you feel comfortable answering, or gives you time to think about questions you don't feel comfortable with.

If you are asked a question about material you have not yet covered, explain when in your program you will be covering that subject. If you are not addressing that topic, explain why not.

When faced with too many questions, have a ready response to regain control of the program. Mine is, "I appreciate your interest, and if time permits, we will select a few more questions before we end."

When you throw a question out to the audience, allow any answer you get back to have validity. Don't compete with the audience. Never make them feel foolish (as they might have felt in school when they did not have the right answer).

To better understand a question, paraphrase the question rather than repeating it before jumping in with an answer. This is an effective method for minimizing skepticism or hostility.

Listen carefully as you're being asked a question, and maintain eye contact with that person. Refrain from interrupting and answering before the person has finished speaking. Then address your answer to the entire audience.

During a workshop or sales presentation, you may find it advantageous to answer questions throughout the presentation. But if you do this, you must take extra care to stay on track and on schedule.

Be aware that some people make sweeping generalities when they ask a question. When this happens, do not answer without first qualifying the question.

When answering a challenging question, offer facts and be diplomatic.

If someone asks you a hostile question, don't match the tone or become angry and defensive. This is the time to show that you can listen to another point of view. Use the "repeat, reflect, and respond" formula.

When someone asks you an argumentative question, answer it quickly and then immediately move on to another question. Don't allow the argument to begin.

Avoid verbal traps, such as, "Do you not agree?" or "Would you not concur?" Rephrasing the question will allow you to maintain control and avoid being manipulated.

If you are asked a question that you are not prepared to answer, simply respond with one of the following:

"I will gather information and get back to you."

"I have that information on my desk. Could you see me after the session?"

"That answer requires more detail than time allows."

"That is an excellent question and worthy of further evaluation."

"I will be happy to discuss that with you after further details are examined."

"Does anyone think they have the answer to that question?" By redirecting the question back to the audience, you may be lucky and someone will know the answer. You can nod in agreement as if you knew the answer all along.

Or you can simply state that you do not have that answer, but indicate a willingness to find the answer after the presentation, as in, "That question cannot be answered briefly. Please see me after the presentation, and I will make time for you."

If you definitely do not have an answer, it is best to be honest. State that you do not know, and show a willingness to find that information or redirect the question to the audience.

Never make fun of a question that has been asked. Getting a laugh by embarrassing someone in your audience is rude.

There are occasions when members of the audience resent the speaker, especially if there is controversy involved in the topic. They want to challenge the speaker, show that they know more than the speaker or just take the attention away from the presentation. If you know in advance there will be conflict and strong differing opinions, acknowledge the controversy at the beginning of your speech and thank them for their courtesy in giving you the opportunity to offer your views.

How do you answer an angry person in your audience? Allow that person to vent his or her emotions, within reason, and then answer in a calm voice. An angry audience can distort your answers and your intentions, and become verbally abusive. So remain calm, composed and open. Keep your face and your body language relaxed. (Do not put your hands on your hips or cross your arms in front of you). Don't point at the audience in a scolding manner. Keep your voice energized and modulated.

Avoid asking, "Did I answer your question?" The audience might say no. This could make you appear incompetent.

Anticipate questions. Politicians, CEOs, and celebrities never appear on national television without being primed. Prior to being interviewed, a politician's aide or an executive's assistant identifies most of the questions likely to be asked. You can do this too. Consider the issues that you will be presenting. Request a colleague to ask you challenging questions. Make a list of the questions that you hope no one will ask, and then prepare answers for them anyway.

Don't exceed your time limits. The audience will become restless and will quit listening.

Try not to call on the same person repeatedly or take questions from only one part of the room.

When you are asked a question that has already been asked and answered, reword it and answer it again. Avoid saying "I have already answered that," or "The answer is obvious; everyone should know that." Your audience will resent you.

The long-winded question can trigger a filibuster situation where someone wants center stage. You must regain control of the session. Don't wait for them to finish. Answer when they pause to take a breath, or ask them to state their question. Remind them that it's only a one-hour (or whatever) program, and scheduling forces you to move on.

If no questions are asked, prepare some in advance. When you ask, "Are there any questions?" pause briefly and then say, "This is a question that is frequently asked." This often breaks the barrier and questions arise. If not, go immediately to your final close.

Yes, from time to time, you will be asked an embarrassing or personal question. Have a stock response. My answer is: "That question is mind over matter, so if you don't mind, it doesn't matter."

If you are speaking to a large audience and you are audio taping your presentation, be sure to repeat all questions into the microphone so the questions are recorded along with the answers.

If you prefer to have questions at the end of your presentation rather than throughout (because you want to develop all of your points fully, or you may feel that questions during the presentation could distract you), tell the audience at the beginning to hold their questions and that you will save time at the end for them. That gives you more control and you can limit the Q&A to your comfort zone. If it is a technical presentation, you may want to take the questions throughout so that there is full clarification on each point.

Don't start packing your gear and folding your notes while the audience is asking questions. Those gestures signal a lack of interest in answering their questions.

If someone asks two questions at once, choose the one you want to answer and then go on to the next person.

When presented with a question that I think the audience can and wants to answer, I throw it open to the audience. It involves the audience, and the question still gets answered.

When you want to end the Q&A, simply thank the audience for their questions. Now you can present your final message, statement, or transparency along with a conclusion to end the session.

Being able to field questions effectively enhances your credibility. A reporter once asked Robert Kennedy at a press conference, "How did you earn the right to become Attorney General of the United States?" Bobby offered his boyish grin and said, "I had a good education, excellent experience in my field... and my brother happens to be President of the United States." The press enjoyed his quick wit and continued with respectful questions.

PREPARE FOR PITFALLS

"You must learn from the mistakes of others; you couldn't possibly live long enough to make them all yourself."

— Sam Levenson

As you know, it is not a perfect world. Even with the best preparation, something can go wrong. I hope this list of remedies gathered from professional speakers will be helpful to you.

Don't ignore noise and distractions outside your meeting room. Instead, send someone to investigate. If it is music or laughter coming from the next room, ask them to tone it down.

Always turn your wireless microphone off when taking a break; otherwise it will amplify your private conversation, telephone call, or visit to the bathroom.

Hecklers in the audience? At first, ignore it. If the distraction continues, try to involve the culprit. Finally, confront the offender and, without anger, ask for cooperation as a consideration for the others in the audience. If things get out of control, stop. And when they throw tomatoes, duck!

You may plan thoroughly, but embarrassing moments can still occur. Life is full of gremlins that appear and say "got ya!" Some problems turn out humorous; others may become a signature story. You will live through them, and your audience will be more responsive to you because of your vulnerability. If a situation has become difficult, call for a 10 minute break, even it is isn't scheduled. That may give you the time to recover or solve the problem.

You have gone "blank," lost your train of thought, and can't remember your next line. Just look at your audience and say one of these phrases:

"Now let's review."

"Let me check my notes to make sure I have covered that point."

"Before we continue, I want to repeat my last point." (Then review your notes.)

This will give you the time to scan your notes and get back on track There is nothing wrong with saying to your audience, "I just forgot what I was going to say, totally lost my thought. So much for a photographic memory." Your audience will understand, it has happened to all of us, in conversations and in front of an audience. Say something - do not just stand there in silence, repeat something you have already said, tell them what you have prepared in the rest of the speech. As you speak, you will remember what you were going to say.

You garble a sentence, your tongue gets twisted, or you fumble with a word. You might say, "Oops, it's a fish, and I'm floundering," or "I'll try that again in English," or, "Shall I translate?"

The microphone squeals. Step away from the microphone and say, "I'm hooked up to outer space," or "They're launching another missile." The problem occurs because your microphone is too close to the amplifier's speakers.

You stumble and fall on stage. If you are not hurt, you can be humorous and say "Now for my next act..." or "See why I am not a dancer?" or "It was love at first sight. I fell for you."

Someone presents a verbal trap. Don't get lost in semantics and double negatives. Don't agree with a question you don't understand.

Sleepers. Ignore them. Unless the person snores out loud or falls off the chair, the audience doesn't notice. Sleeping can be the result of antihistamines, fatigue, or illness, so don't take it personally; it happens to all of us.

The audience opposes your views. State at the beginning, "I am aware that many of you differ with my point of view. I appreciate your courtesy in giving me the opportunity to express my feelings."

Someone asks a rude question. You don't have to answer every question. Either say, "That is not appropriate at this time," or ignore it and go on to another question or resume your presentation.

The equipment fails. Tell the audience that your worst nightmare finally came true, and ask if a technically oriented person in the audience can help. If possible, proceed on another track in a different format.

Never underestimate the ability of the audience to misinterpret what you say. Keith L. Flake, speaking to the inmates of the Arizona State Penitentiary stated, "It's good to see you all here. I'm pleased to have such a captive audience."

It is against the copyright laws to use music, recordings, or cartoons without an authorized license agreement. It's theft. It's illegal. Don't do it.

If you are presenting during a meal, request the food service be completed before you begin to speak. Waiters make a lot of noise and aren't concerned with what you have to say, especially when they are clearing dishes to finish their shift. Make sure that you make your request to the person in charge. Also request that if the kitchen is nearby, the waiters don't hold loud conversations that can be heard in the diningroom.

If you are at a restaurant that has piped in Muzak, ask that it be turned off during your speech.

You may be asked to speak for a specific length of time, such as thirty minutes. You are told that no matter what happens, you must end your speech by 1:30. The speaker before you takes additional time and you are introduced at 1:15 pm. You have prepared and rehearsed for a thirty minute speech. What do you do? Open with a smile. Begin with your opening statement, cut to your main point, offer support statements, add a good story or example and go to your summation. You will be a hero.

Even if you're "on a roll," end your presentation on schedule. If you go over time, your audience will become restless and begin to resent you.

A member of the audience begins a filibuster, mainly because they want to show how much they know or they just like the limelight. You must regain control. Say: "Just one moment, let me answer that," and proceed to provide an answer. Then quickly call on someone else so that person does not reclaim the floor

The Eager Beaver always wants to answer all the questions first, to show how much he knows. Say: "Thanks for your answers. Now let's give others in the audience an opportunity."

Don't try to be all things to all people and speak only on a subject that you know well or have time to research.

You have come down with a cold the night before a big speech. Your eyes are burning, your throat is sore, your nose is red and running. Avoid alcohol, iced drinks, smoke. Run the shower with hot water and allow the steam to fill up the room with you in it. Drink warm tea or soup. Take Zicam spray (non-prescription) Sleep propped up with two large pillows. In the morning take a non-drowsy anti-histamine, more hot tea, have throat lozenges, Visine and tissues handy.

Always have "Plan B" ready. Expect the unexpected. Prepare, rehearse, and have a contingency plan. Remember, speaking is a form of show business.

Common mistakes:

Not arriving early • Lacking enthusiasm • Not caring about your audience's needs • Not rehearsing• Reading your speech • Using too many overheads • Not using examples and stories • Forgetting about your non-verbal messages • Trying to please everyone

QUICK REVIEW

MAKE USE OF THE PAUSE, IT'S SPEAKING PUNCTUATION

USE VOCAL VARIETY TO AVOID A MONOTONE

TONE, PITCH AND VOLUME SPEAK FOR YOU

INTERACT WITH YOUR AUDIENCE

INVOLVE YOUR AUDIENCE TO PARTICIPATE

ARRANGE GROUP INTER-ACTION

ICE BRAKERS

KEEP COOL WHEN ANSWERING DIFFICULT QUESTIONS

REVIEW SOLUTIONS FOR PITFALLS

Part 6

LEADERSHIP, PROMOTING YOURSELF, EARN MONEY AS A PAID SPEAKER

"Don't wait for your ship to come in, swim out to meet it."

LEADERSHIP, SELF-PROMOTION, EARN MONEY AS A PAID SPEAKER

QUALITIES OF LEADERSHIP

What is leadership? How do you become a leader? *Why* should you become a leader? Let's consider the last question first.

Leadership isn't just about being the boss. When you acquire leadership skills, you open the door to many opportunities — promotion in your work, a chance to advance and be recognized in your industry, and the prospect of making a difference in your community. Simply put, leadership is the path to your own success.

Leadership begins with the ability to express your ideas to other people, and to sell yourself to achieve your goals. A good leader can conduct meetings and teach, train, and council others. Leadership qualities allow you to network with others for resources, referrals and references. When necessary, a leader has to rise to the occasion of being interviewed, possibly on video and be ready to express ideas and communicate with many different types of people.

I realize that you may not want to be the president of a corporation or the director of a major expedition. But acquiring leadership skills does mean that you will appear more experienced and more valuable to your industry. You will be perceived by others as influential. When a person demonstrates leadership, they have an advantage over people that shy away from responsibility. You can display leadership qualities and be a leader without assuming authority or having an actual title.

Being a leader *does* require that you:

- Develop a vision and be able to express it
- Have authentic values and ethics
- Express your purpose and principles with passion

- Encourage and help others meet their goals
- Admit your mistakes, and criticize others only in private
- Practice the art of listening, and be open and accessible to others
- Allow calculated risk taking into your life
- Be adaptable to change
- Adopt the ability to communicate with people of diverse styles and cultures
- Show enthusiasm, and remain optimistic

In the business arena, we are all in sales either selling an idea, a service, or a product. This is true whether or not we think of ourselves as salespeople. We need the ability to sell ourselves to others, and convince them that we can handle the task, or provide the service or goods that they want.

In the same way, you need leadership skills, whether or not you call yourself a "leader." The way that you project and express yourself will determine your success. If you want to make a difference in your community, at work, as part of a team, or as a role model for your family, you need leadership skills.

In his bestselling book *Leadership,* Rudolph Giuliani states, "A leader must not only set direction, but must communicate that direction. To bring people aboard, you must excite them with your vision and earn their support. Leaders communicate in a way that inspires. Preparation is a key element to success." Leadership is certainly a skill Giuliani has in abundance.

The first parts of this book have focused on developing your presentation skills. Now it's time to give you the tools to extend your presentation skills into leadership skills.

We'll begin with the leadership role of conducting a meeting. A checklist will guide you through all the steps required to make your meeting successful and help keep you in control of the group.

The next area we'll focus on is self-promotion, because part of leadership is being able to network, meet people, and expand your sphere of influence.

The final step of leadership is to be able to mentor, coach, train and council people. You can see that all of the earlier parts of this book have been building your communication skills so that you can step into a leadership role.

First, let's look at the leadership skills required to run a successful meeting.

HOW TO CONDUCT A SUCCESSFUL MEETING

You are the one chosen to conduct the meeting, are you more than pleased? Or is it your worst nightmare? Would you rather go to the dentist and have your teeth drilled? It could turn out like most meetings — disorganized, boring, full of conflicts, and not achieving much. Or you could arrange a meeting that is structured, efficient, and produces results. It's up to you. Productive meetings don't just happen. They are the result of planning and preparation.

The successful meeting begins with a prepared, organized and realistic agenda. The agenda should not be so rigid that it inhibits creativity and participation. Most meetings start late, last too long, and don't achieve the desired goals. The result is that another meeting is required which means more time, energy and effort. An agenda will help you avoid many of the common pitfalls.

The following guidelines will assist you in planning and conducting a successful meeting.

Ask yourself, is this meeting even necessary? What is its purpose? What is its goal? Are you holding it simply because you always have a meeting on Tuesday morning?

Prepare a realistic agenda. Identify the most important points to be discussed on the top of the list. Who are the individuals most involved in each point? Does each point involve discussion or a decision? An agenda keeps everyone on track and allows them to see what needs to be accomplished.

Where will the meeting take place? A board room with a rectangle table? A classroom? An office? Plan the room arrangement for maximum effectiveness. Is it the right size to accommodate the amount of people attending? How do you want the chairs arranged? Are tables needed for writing? Is the room well lit?

Does everyone have directions to the location of the meeting?

Do you need to consider special needs for participants with disabilities, language barriers and lower educational levels?

People have preconceived, and usually negative, ideas about "meetings," so call it something else. Be creative! *Call it an event, a think tank, a summit, an idea exchange, a micro-meeting, a modular meeting, a track meet, a retreat, or an orientation.*

Inform participants of the agenda in advance, along with the projected time frames. This gives them the opportunity to prepare any materials or reports.

Involve participants as early as possible. Give them a feeling of ownership in the meeting and its outcome. If possible the agenda could be prepared collaboratively using an electronic network. It can be reviewed and prioritized in advance. This will enable participants to be prepared. Your meeting can be information sharing rather than information pile-up

Before the meeting, pre-assign segments of the meeting to participants for them to coordinate. This will insure their involvement.

Have name tags available.

Open the meeting on a positive note with a welcoming statement. Plan self introductions or an icebreaker to put everyone at ease.

Realize that people attending a meeting come with their own agendas, different personality styles, and different values. That is why it is important to specify the purpose and goals of the meeting and keep it focused.

Serve juice and veggies ("think tank" food) rather than coffee and donuts.

Track the cost and expenses of your meeting, including the time and money involved in keeping participants away from their desks or from serving customers.

Learn to read your participants' body language. Do they understand you?

Do they agree with you? Are they asking valid questions? Do they look bored or hostile? Are you encouraging participants to express their opinions?

End with a summary of the meeting and a proposal for further activities.

Finally, be sure to thank the participants for their time, ideas, and suggestions.

NEW TECHNOLOGY FOR MEETINGS

Be aware of the ways that technology is changing the very nature of meetings. For example, consider the way that video-conferencing enables people in different geographical locations to attend the same meeting. And rather than having participants come together for training, video-conferencing brings distance learning to them.

According to the *Wall Street Journal*, video-conferencing has tripled every year since 2002. Consequently, meeting facilities are increasing their capability for video-conferencing. Many hotels have installed systems in meeting rooms. Small room video conference systems have become more affordable

Dr. Terrie Temkin, President of Non-Profit Management Solutions, Inc, an international consulting firm specializing in governance and board development (see resources), often recommends her clients use Web conferencing. Such technology allows organizations to recruit the best and the brightest to serve on board or committees, since people can participate in real-time meetings at minimal cost regardless of where in the world they reside. Temkin warns, however, that organizations must first confirm that their state statutes and their own organizational bylaws permit the use of this technology when making decisions. Also, she suggests continuing to hold the occasional person to person meeting to enhance thrust and build a sense of "groupness." If that is not possible, posting pictures of the participants helps.

The newest setups are available with Image Tracking Systems, which allow cameras to follow the person being videotaped without requiring the constant presence of a videographer The cameras have zoom, tilt and pan capabilities.

Many organizations are instituting board meetings via e-mail, chat rooms, or other Internet-based communications methods. These approaches save travel time, but there are drawbacks — participants cannot simultaneously hear each other, limiting real communication.

The impact of "virtual meetings" is undeniable. However, video-conferencing and Internet-based meetings are not particularly effective for building relationships, so they are not going to completely replace traditional meetings anytime soon.

Think of webcasting as a form of television, a one way transmission via the Internet. It can be used for large or small groups that require limited interaction. Webconferencing is directed at smaller groups and provides application sharing, Web touring and whiteboard annotation. Basically it comes down to Webcast for active video but limited interaction and webconference for interaction but limited video.

Whatever the format and venue of your meeting, as the chairperson of the meeting you are the facilitator — not the monopolizer — of the discussion. Part of your leadership responsibility is to encourage participation from everyone. For example, when attendees ask you questions, you should redirect those questions back to the group whenever possible.

It is also your responsibility to run an orderly meeting. Establish time frames for your meeting and stick to them. Become familiar with Robert's Rules (parliamentary procedure) to help maintain order. Maintain a calm demeanor if conflicts arise. Attempt to resolve the differences, but do not take sides in the debate.

Your responsibilities for the meeting begin long before the actual starting time. You should plan ahead for your administrative needs and staff requirements. You might need to keep budget considerations in mind, such as the costs of food, beverages, service, and meeting room rental. Travel arrangements might be your responsibility, along with the preparation and printing of workbooks and handout materials. If some of your participants are traveling to your meeting, you need to consider hotel accommodations and ground transportation.

Audiovisual support is your responsibility, including rental of audiovisual equipment, microphones, flipcharts, a projector, a screen, video monitors, and even the room lighting. Finally, be in contact with your hired speakers and prepare for their honorarium payment, pre-meeting requests, arrival, and comfort.

Your responsibilities continue after the meeting has ended. A summary of the meeting needs to be prepared and distributed to everyone concerned — both those who attended the meeting, and the people who missed it.

Rather than writing lengthy minutes, create a summary chart of the meeting's activities, with one-line descriptions of the items discussed. The summary should list the decisions made, the actions to be taken, or the individuals responsible for the actions. Keeping informal notes will enable the information to be used for future meetings.

According to research conducted by the American Society for Training and Development, over eleven *million* meetings take place in the United States every day. No wonder I can never reach anyone on the phone. They are all in meetings! At least that's what their voicemail tells me

In addition to the preceding insights and suggestions, the following check-lists and forms will help you keep your meetings on track.

STOP "CHAIRING THE BORED"

A leader controls the meeting by:

Beginning the meeting with enthusiasm.

Identifying and defining problems.

Stating the purpose of the meeting.

Preparing a realistic agenda.

Stimulating an exchange of ideas.

Remaining impartial during conflict and stressing. cooperation between disagreeing parties.

Acknowledging the needs of participants and their physical comfort.

Clarifying the meeting's objectives and summarizing frequently.

Targeting a task or goal.

Providing an action plan.

Delegating responsibilities.

Merging different personality styles to work as a team.

Creating a follow-up or benchmark of activities to be performed.

Encouraging active participation.

Maintaining a positive mode.

Building a team mentality by using the word "we" rather than "I".

Specifying how the decision-making process works.

Closing on a positive note and thanking the participants for attending.

Reviewing and evaluating the meeting.

Maintaining a written or recorded transcript of the meeting.

MEETING CHECKLIST:

Meeting date:

Location:

Meeting notice distributed:

Participants:

Starting time:

Room reserved:

Chair arrangement:

Meeting materials: notepads, pencils, name badges, manuals

Equipment: flipchart, marking pens, microphone, slide projector, spare bulb, screen, projector table, lectern, overhead projector, video monitor, computer

Minutes recorded by:

Agenda:

Objectives:

Food and beverage:

Review and results of meeting:

Follow-up action

Minutes distributed to participants

MEETING NOTICE:

A MEETING IS SCHEDULED

Date:
       To:

Date of meeting   Time:

Location: Directions:

Purpose of meeting:

Materials and preparation:

Enclosed: Copy of meeting agenda
               Required data
               Resource materials

Please confirm that you have received this notice and will be able to attend.

Roger Smith
Phone: (318) 775-3902
Fax: (318) 775-3922
email: car@net.com

MEETING ACTION PLAN

Meeting Date:

Meeting Chairman:

Participants:

Recorder:

KEY ISSUES:

IDEAS AND SUGGESTIONS

ACTION PLAN:

DATE BEGIN:
DATE OF COMPLETION:

NEXT MEETING DATE:

ISSUES:

MAINTAINING CONTROL AND DEALING WITH DIFFICULT PERSONALITIES

As you conduct meetings, you may find that some people put you into difficult situations. Here are some ideas that you can use to handle these challenging people, and keep order and control of the meeting.

The Latecomers

They always arrive late.

Solution: Begin your meeting on time, and don't start over to accommodate the latecomer. They'll learn.

The Get-Up-And-Go People

They always leave before the conclusion of the meeting.

Solution: Be sure the meeting notice states the length of the meeting. Underline that it's each person's responsibility to arrange his or her schedule to remain until the conclusion of the meeting.

The Non-participators

They are quiet and unresponsive.

Solution: Ask their opinions on issues and draw them into the discussion by asking open-ended questions. Pre-assign information for them to present at the meeting.

The Limelighters

They have a lot to say and enjoy being in the center stage.

They are seeking recognition. They cannot be allowed to take control and use your meeting for their showcase, so thank them for their interest and then point out that you also want to get responses from everyone in the group and that there is limited time for the meeting.

The Broken Records

They bring up the same point over and over. They tend to be over analytical and probe into unnecessary details.

Solution: Inform them that you will supply the details *after* the meeting. Remind them that spending too much time on one point would disrupt the schedule for the remainder of the meeting. Refer to your notes and to any previous minutes to see if the issue has already been discussed. Announce that it is important to continue with the agenda at hand.

The Always Negatives

They disagree with everything, all of the time. They feel that any discussion is a waste of time. They pull down the energy level of a meeting.

Solution: Ask them to suspend judgment until everything has been discussed. Remind everyone to be open to new ideas and to target positive approaches to solving problems.

The Hostile Attackers

They offer strong disagreement (usually in a loud voice) and they take pride in their displays of anger. They want an argument.

Solution: Allow them to vent their feelings, but do not mirror their angry posture and tone. Don't shout back — the anger will just escalate and the meeting could get out of control. (This is what the attacker would like to see.) Respond in a calm, controlled voice and return to your agenda. If the meeting becomes disruptive you can ask if everyone to focus on the issues, not personalities. Ask for mutual respect allowing everyone their turn to speak Assure the participants that all interests and concerns will be addressed.

The Side Conversationalists

They hold their own private meetings during your meeting. Even if their voices are low and can't be heard, they're still a distraction. They're not paying attention, which can frustrate and aggravate other participants.

Solution: This can fragment the meeting. Ask that they remain focused on the group's activities and the agenda.

The Cell Phones

They disrupt the meeting when their cell phones ring. (They disrupt the meeting even more if they answer the phone during the meeting.)

Solution: Request that all cell phones be turned off or placed on vibrate. Ask that cell phone conversations take place outside of the meeting room.

The Side Trackers

They wait until the end of the meeting to resurrect issues that have been discussed.

Solution: Listen to their remarks, and then state your regret that they waited until the end of the meeting. Remind them that they did not say anything when the issue was on the floor earlier. Say that it is time to conclude this meeting, and that issue can be raised at another time (unless a decision has been made or an action has been designated).

SELF PROMOTION, MEETING THE PRESS, BEING INTERVIEWED, APPEARING ON VIDEO

"Facing the press is more difficult than bathing a leper."
Mother Teresa

MEET THE PRESS

It can happen when you least expect it. Maybe you witnessed an incident, or you're trying to promote a product or event, or perhaps your opinion is important on a current issue. Suddenly you find a microphone in your face, a camera pointed at you, and questions directed at you.

Your first thoughts probably will be: "Will I have the right answers? Do I have to answer all questions? How do I look?" Sometimes you'll have time to prepare, but other times life is totally spur-of-the-moment. The information in this segment will help you prepare when there is no time to prepare.

If you agree to be interviewed, gather as much information beforehand about the interview as possible. What will be the scope of the interview? How long will the interview last? What will the interview be used for?

When it comes time for the interview, know your objectives and the main points that you want to make. To establish an atmosphere of honesty and truthfulness, maintain eye contact with the person interviewing you, and be sure to address the host or interviewer by name.

You can't control all of the questions an interviewer will ask. However, there are techniques that you can use to prepare and safeguard your responses in the interview. They include:

Listen carefully to the questions. Take a few seconds to think before you answer.

Tell yourself to look and act calm and at ease. Drop your shoulders and arms, and relax your facial muscles. If you look confident, it will add to your credibility.

Avoid sounding defensive by using a controlled and reasonable voice, but feel free to correct any negative statements that are thrown at you.

If two people ask questions at the same time, choose one to answer.

Mention your company, your product, or your main point as early as possible in the interview.

If the interviewer should ask at the end of the interview, "Any final comments?" or "Is there anything you would like to add?" be ready with a zinger of a closing statement and drive home the point of your main issue.

Avoid replying "no comment." That statement, like "pleading the fifth," gives the impression that you are hiding something. If answering a question infringes on company confidentiality or legally it would be a problem to answer, say so. You can offer a response like, "That question will be answered at the appropriate time," or "There is not enough time at this point to fully answer the question." Explaining why you can't answer at this time makes you look more confident.

If you don't like the question being asked, field and fog by answering with a different point that you want to bring up. Politicians do that all the time. You can say, "That is an interesting question, but what I really find of great importance is...."

Be careful not to endorse a paraphrase of your remark. It could be a trap and change the meaning of what you said.

When you have time to prepare, ask yourself — what is your message? Who is the audience? What is your main point? What are the benefits? What are the results that you seek? Can you express that in short sound bites?

Remember, the news media is not in business to make you look good. They couldn't care less. They are looking for headlines or articles to grab their readers attention. The news media is not interested in enhancing your business, only in covering an informative and entertaining story. Although, fair journalist will show both sides of an issue. You may find yourself portrayed in an unflattering manner, so be sure to have damage control plans in position before going into an interview.

Avoid inflammatory remarks. When a professor from Miami referred to his city as a "banana republic" on ABC's *60 Minutes*, he had to spend the next two weeks explaining to an angry community what he really meant. And even then he was not forgiven.

Avoid talking too much, too fast, or with too much excitement. Try to remain poised and in control.

If you will be using a Teleprompter, familiarize yourself with the script beforehand. Such preparation will eliminate the perception of obvious reading, which makes your delivery seem insincere. Also it will give the Teleprompter operator an opportunity to judge the speed at which you speak, so the prompter can scroll at a comfortable pace.

Assume that the camera is on you at all times. Even when you are not speaking, the camera may be getting a reaction shot of you. If someone else is speaking, you may still be in the frame. Don't let your guard down and look disinterested.

Assume the microphone is still on at the end of the taping. While the credits are scrolling, your words may still be heard. You will also be on camera while the credits are scrolling, so stay attentive. Don't crumble with relief that it is over, don't giggle, and don't jump up from the seat. At the end of the show, turn to the host, smile, and engage in quiet conversation.

Remember nothing is "off the record." Avoid negative responses. Turn negative questions into positive replies. Be prepared for an opposing point of view. Avoid the "what if" questions that reporters love to ask.

Send your media kit in advance. Include your biography, background material on your business, reference letters, press releases of past events, and points that you would like to discuss during the interview.

Arrive at the studio early enough to meet the interviewer (although sometimes they don't show up until the last minute) and to become comfortable with the surroundings. See the stage and where you will be placed. If you are in a chair, you will be told not to move it, because it is positioned for the camera. They will attach a microphone to you by clipping it on your clothes and putting the cord under your clothes. Let them do their job; don't waste time being modest. (Sometimes they place the microphone on your body with duct tape. Ouch!) Maybe you will meet the host, or maybe not. The hot lights go on. The smiling host arrives and it begins SHOW TIME! I hope that you have the interview on tape to see afterwards, because you probably won't remember a thing you said. In some ways, being on a TV show is like being anesthetized for outpatient surgery — you don't remember anything afterwards.

Don't bring notes. You are the expert, and you know what message you want to get across to the audience. Notes diminish your credibility.

If your product or service is going to be mentioned, ask the producer before the show if your contact number can be superimposed on the screen. It makes it easier for people to order from you.

Request a list of questions that you will be asked, and review them ahead of time.

Meet the floor director. He will explain helpful information like the hand signals for "on the air." He'll also tell you which camera is focused on you, and when you are off the air.

Check the video monitor to see how you look.

Find out ahead of time whether the show will be broadcast live or taped for a later showing.

Ask the producer if they will be recording a tape of the interview. You can then supply your own tape — DAT (digital audiotape) or CDR (compact disk recordable). If you want a copy of the show bring an extra tape to be dubbed.

What is the format of the program? Find out the length of your segment and when the breaks occur. Will there be other guests? Find out who they are and how they fit into the program.

If it is a taped interview and not live, the reporter may spend as long as 1/2 hour with you. But not everything you say may make it to the air. After the footage is edited, you may be featured for ten minutes, or maybe only three minutes. Or just thirty seconds. So use ten-second sound bites to get your points in quickly.

Plan in advance to present your views in short direct sentences — get right to the point quickly, and then elaborate if you have the time.

Use simple declarative sentences. Avoid one word answers. If you say "yes" or "no," use it as a bridge to get another point across.

Look directly at the person interviewing you, and listen attentively to what they're saying.

Relax your facial muscles; don't look apprehensive.

Anticipate the questions that you may be asked, and rehearse your answers.

If you are uncertain of a question's meaning, ask to have it be repeated or clarified.

When you're on a panel, stay focused — even when the question isn't directed to you. You don't always know when the camera is focused on you, so don't yawn, scratch, or look bored.

If you are presenting a provocative or controversial topic, be sure that you can defend your ideas.

GETTING ON A TALK SHOW

How do you get asked to be a guest on a television show? First, recognize that television producers are looking for news, useful information, anything related to current events or trends, and human interest stories. They do not want to give you the opportunity to sell your product and use their time for a commercial.

If you have something that you feel is newsworthy, an effective method of bringing it to the media's attention is to send press releases to the newspapers and television show producers. Give details of your news event, your key points, and the thrust of your message and how it relates to their audience. Position yourself as an expert or a specialist.

After you've sent your press release to the program director of the station or the producer of a particular show, follow up with an email, and then a phone call. If you don't want to do it yourself, you can hire a PR firm. They know all the ways to promote you and they have the contacts to the right people.

TELEPHONE INTERVIEW

If you're being interviewed by phone, be sure you're in a quiet place where you can talk without interruptions. You should talk on a regular (landline) phone, not a cell phone. Be sure that your "call waiting" signal is turned off. Also make sure that you won't be interrupted by ringing doorbells or somebody picking up an extension to make a call. Keep a glass of water nearby in case your throat gets dry.

CHECKLIST FOR A TV INTERVIEW

1) Sit straight. Use good posture. Keep your knees together. Avoid gripping the armrest of the chair so tightly that your knuckles turn white.

2) If you are seated, unbutton your jacket. If you are standing, button your jacket.

3) Be concise, and get your key points across right at the beginning.

4) Remember to look sincere and direct when you face the camera. There is a difference between looking into the eye of a camera that offers no response, and looking out at an audience that is constantly giving you feedback with their eyes and body language. You must keep in mind that there is a living, breathing audience — you just can't see them.

5) On video, use fewer gestures and remain in one area of the stage. Prepare for the various camera angles. The camera may move in for a close up of your face. Remember, eye contact is important, whether it is with the camera or your interviewer.

6) Write your contact information on a sticky note and give it to the receptionist. If your appearance generates calls to the studio, she'll have the information near her phone

7) At the end of the taping, thank the host for inviting you.

CLOTHES AND COLORS FOR VIDEO

Dressing correctly for video is even more important than dressing correctly when you're on-stage. Always dress conservatively. You want people to remember the outrageous things you say, not the outrageous way you look.

Remember that bright colors become more intense onscreen. Red or bright orange can create a glare. White and black play havoc with the lighting — white reflects too much light and black is too flat, so wear ivory or dark gray instead. Other colors that work well include: blue, beige, camel, mauve, apricot, peach, and navy.

Be careful of the clothes you choose. Bulky and baggy clothes make you look large. Busy patterns, small prints, large plaids, and herringbone patterns tend to shimmer on video. Shiny fabrics and metallic jewelry drive video technicians crazy because the shine causes light flares.

TV studio lights are extremely bright, and they wash out skin color and create a shine. So bring some Kleenex tissues with you to the studio, along with some translucent powder to eliminate shine on your nose, forehead, and the top of your head (if you are bald). Apply the powder with a powder puff or powder brush, being careful not to spill powder onto your navy suit.

Women should always wear foundation, blush, mascara and lipstick. Avoid purple, hot pink or brown lipsticks — those colors make your teeth look yellow. Be sure all your makeup is blended (without streaks) on your face Avoid glossy iridescent cosmetics. Bring your own comb, brush, hair spray and lint brush.

Men should shave just prior to appearing on TV because the overhead lighting can create a five o'clock shadow. The lighting can also create shadows under the eyes, so use a makeup stick (in a medium shade) under the eyes and blend it well. Use a light bronzer if you need to acquire an instant tan.

It's a good idea to always have eye drops with you in case a contact lens gets stuck or your eyes are red and dry from lack of sleep. If you wear eyeglasses with shiny metal glass frames, touch them lightly with a little beige foundation to eliminate glare. Don't wear tinted glasses. Also, be sure that your hair is not covering your eyes or casting a shadow on your eyes. If your hair covers your eyebrows, it is too long.

When it comes to makeup, less is better. If you are pale and require a good coverage of foundation on your face and neck, it's a good idea to apply a thin coat of makeup to the back of your hands also. This stops your white hands from clashing with your tanned face. If you should smear makeup on a white collar, rub some white chalk on it to absorb the oil. If at all possible, it's best to have a professional makeup artist apply your makeup for you.

PROFESSIONAL SPEAKING, MARKETING, PUBLICITY AND NETWORKING

EARN MONEY AS A PAID SPEAKER

I constantly receive calls from people who say they want to become professional speakers. They ask questions like, "How do I get started?" "How do you acquire speaking engagements?" "Who hires you?" "What can I charge?"

I answer with my own questions — "Do you have something to talk about? What is your area of expertise? What are you passionate about? What do you have to offer? What kind of audience wants to hear your message?"

Professional speakers speak on a wide variety of subjects and topics. For instance, my major area of expertise is communication skills. Under that umbrella are my specialties — Customer Service, Networking, and Speaking Skills.

It is important to become a specialist, learn everything on your topic and stay current with industry trends and changes. You can only feel confident as a speaker if you have taken the time to develop a background, expertise and interesting information in your field.

What speaking topics are popular? Donna Horkey, President of Missing Link Consultants, Inc. (see Resources page) is also past director of the Human Resource Directors of Florida. Donna states, "The most recent trends in training programs are leadership skills, executive development and coaching. Human resource directors view the ability to articulate ideas and generate enthusiasm as a vital part of leadership skill development. Many training departments outsource their trainers from independent companies."

So how do you get started? First, you need to decide on your speaking topic, your own area of expertise. Once you have selected your topic, you need to become a specialist on that subject. Research and read everything that you can find on that topic.

Once you are an authority on your subject, you can go in a variety of directions — you can develop a training seminar or workshop, you can offer coaching or consulting. You can write articles for trade magazines or self publish a book on your topic. Your marketing can begin with contacting oganizations and associations that would benefit from your experience and knowledge. The material you have developed will expand as you constantly research and stay current in your field.

The difference between a seminar and a workshop is very slight. It is described in part one of this book. Basically, a workshop is more "hands on" than a seminar. Coaching and consulting overlap. Coaching is usually one-on-one, similar to mentoring, consulting is more in-depth within an industry.

My company, The Training Express, combines training, consulting and coaching. We work with small and large businesses, major corporations and individuals, therefore we have to be flexible. The goal of our company is to put employees, managers and the CEO on the right track toward leadership and customer service.

One company may be a training workshop for their sales staff on presentation skills, a customer service seminar for their entire company. Another company may want consulting services on leadership and professional image for mid and upper management. This would involve a detailed needs assessment on the part of our company to understand their goals. There are times when the CEO and top executives want to have a higher comfort level when addressing their staff, speaking in public,answering questions or appearing on video. That would come under the heading of coaching. Once you have knowledge, expertise and are a specialist, you can deliver all of those formats to your client.

Do you believe in free speech? Well, that's where it all begins — speaking without getting paid. Start networking at local Chambers of Commerce events, approach various business associations, and go to business card exchanges in your area. Rotary Clubs, Kiwanis Clubs, and hundreds of business and professional groups hold regular meetings — and they are always looking for speakers!

Unfortunately, they normally do not have a budget for speakers, so you won't get paid (at least, not in money). You will receive a free lunch or dinner, and sometimes a plaque or some other small trophy with the organization's name. Although you're not receiving a fee, this is an excellent method to gain experience in front of an audience. And if your program goes well, you can ask for a testimonial letter (written on the organization's letterhead) that you can use in your press kit.

Every time you offer a "gratis" speech, you gain experience, meet new people, and get the opportunity for "spin off" engagements.

Along with speaking for free, begin to network with organizations that hire speakers and trainers such as Meeting Professionals International, the American Society of Association Executives, and the American Society for Training and Development. (see resource page) These associations have local chapters throughout the United States.

Toastmasters International is another organization you should join. They don't hire speakers, but they are dedicated to helping people develop their speaking skills. The National Speakers Association also provides an excellent opportunity to network and learn marketing skills from others that earn their living as full time speakers, trainers and consultants.

Through the magic of the Internet, now you can even attend a "speaker's school," regardless of where you live. In his Free-2-Fee Professional Speaker's Coaching Program (www.Free2Fee.com), Jim Barber has condensed his quarter-century of experience as a professional speaker into an easy-to-follow, affordable on-line coaching program for people who want to enter the exciting — and profitable — world of professional speaking. If you want to be paid for expressing your views, Jim's program will show you, step by step, exactly how to do it. (Go to www.Free2Fee.com and tell Jim that "Carolyn" sent you!)

If you're going to take your own career seriously, I strongly recommend that you become a member of the "Up Your Fee" Speaker Enrichment Center. You can discover everything you want to know about professional speaking at www.UpYourFee.com

To help launch your speaking career, you need to write a speaker's business plan that defines your objectives and your course of action. You also want to begin to build a database of prospects (future clients). You should also prepare a budget, allocating adequate money for marketing, publicity and office maintenance.

Once you have started speaking for money, you can contact "speakers' bureaus" to represent you. (Note: they are only interested in experienced speakers. Don't waste their time — and yours — by contacting them before you're ready.) Check The International Group of Agencies and Bureaus (IGAB) They are looking for experts or celebrities. There are some bureaus that also provide trainers and conduct workshops for public seminars. Contact Convention & Visitor Bureaus (CVBs), Destination Management Companies, meeting planners, and special event planners. Of course, you must continually network within your target market or industry and with associations that would benefit from your information and expertise.

Most beginning speakers start with an office in their home. Today's "home office essentials" include a fax machine, a computer, a web site and an e-mail address. For more information on setting up a home office read *Home Office Know-How* by Jeffrey D. Zbar. (See Resources page)

MARKETING

If you're going to get paid to speak, networking just isn't enough — you need a well-formulated marketing plan. Some of the tools that you need to start your marketing campaign include:

1) a one-page letter (on professional letterhead stationery) that lists the titles of your speeches

2) a biography

3) a description of what you have to offer, detailing the benefits of hiring you as a speaker

4) your business card

5) a press kit that includes a photo and reference letters from previous speaking engagements

NETWORKING

Networking, meeting people to acquire referrals, references and resources is an important part of marketing. Make up your mind that you are going to attend functions where you may not know a sole in the room. It is up to you to "work the room" meet as many people as you can. Develop a mindset of: we are too old to be shy! My networking workshops on mingle management have turned introverts into networking experts. We show people how to walk up to others, introduce themselves, make conversation, be interested in other people, what their interests are and how you can be of service to them. The object is getting to the point where they have a new comfort level when meeting people and promoting themselves. The most successful net workers are interested in giving rather than receiving. Come prepared with a crisp business card that is easy to read and be able to tell people what you do in a brief and direct manner.

When someone asks you "What do you do?" don't go into a long commercial. That's boring. If you are brief, it is more than likely they will ask to know more. Everyone you meet may qualify to be part of your network, don't prejudge. One of the most important aspects of networking is to follow up on your leads quickly before they become cold.

The whole point of your marketing campaign is to land a paid speaking engagement. Once you have reached a verbal agreement with a client, send a letter of agreement stating all of the parameters of the engagement. Also send a confirmation letter for the engagement, as well as a program checklist to insure all the details are covered. (See the examples on the following pages.)

When you are hired by a meeting planner or program director, they expect you to be able to relate to the audience, be flexible, focus on the topic that they requested, customize your material meet their specific needs, and refrain from selling books or tapes from the platform. The client will certainly like to see you bridge with the audience. You are expected to arrive early and be prepared to speak within the allotted time.

Is it worth it? Yes, being a speaker can be glamorous — sometimes. You travel to exotic places. On occasion, you are met at the airport by a limousine. You find fruit, flowers, and candy in your deluxe suite. You meet interesting people who want to hear what you have to say.

All this, and you receive a lovely check and an endorsement letter at the end.

On the other hand, glamour gets a little thin when you are eating a sandwich in your hotel room in Winnipeg, Canada, watching a snowstorm outside your window... and you didn't bring a coat because it was May. There is even less glamour when you are stuck in a drafty airport, your plane is delayed, and all you want to do is go home.

Moreover, you can't beat the "glamour" of presenting a workshop at 4 p.m. at a beautiful beachfront resort... with an audience that would rather be on the golf course, the beach, the shops, the restaurant, or the pool — almost anyplace but in your seminar.

Despite this, professional speaking is a wonderful career, and I strongly encourage you to consider it. But always remember that the real "star" isn't you... it's the program that you deliver, the information that you provide, and the help that you give people. That's the real joy of being a professional speaker.

SPEAKING ENGAGEMENT CHECKLIST

Date
Organization
Contact Person _____ Phone _____ Fax_____
Address
Location of Program
Phone
Travel arrangements
Topic   _Title
Beginning Time _____ Ending Time _____
Introduction _____ Theme
Number of people expected in audience _____
Demographics of the audience

Room arrangement:
__ Classroom   __ Auditorium   __ Circle
__ Round tables   __ Long tables   __ Boardroom

Equipment: __ Lectern   __ Riser
               __ Wireless microphone
               __ Overhead projector
               __ Screen
               __ Projector table
               __ Flip chart
               __ TV monitor
               __ Markers
               __ Slide projector
               __ Computer
               __ Extension cord
               __ Tape recorder
               __ Workbook
               __ Handouts
               __ Props
               __ Evaluation sheets
               __ Business cards
               __ Invoice
               __ Follow-up afterwards with meeting planner

LETTER OF AGREEMENT

_____, as an independent contractor, agrees to perform the following services.

Program:

Client:
Location:
Date: _____ Time: _____
Investment: _____ Deposit: _____
Terms:
Materials:

The deposit will guarantee the date. Travel arrangements and expenses are to be paid in advance. Payment for services is due and payable no later than the day of the presentation. If you have not received an invoice by the date of the presentation, either the speaker or a staff member will provide a copy.   Please   make   check   payable   to

_____.

If you are in agreement with the above outlined program and fee, please sign and return one copy to _____.

Signed
Signed ——————————————————————————————
       Client   Title   Date

Audio or videotaping is not permitted without expressed and prior permission from the speaker. Please send all publicity concerning the speaker and the program to our office prior to the presentation.

THE TRAVELING SPEAKER—
IN THE AIR, OVER LAND, AT SEA

Speaking internationally is wonderful. I should know — I have had the unique opportunity to present my workshops in Canada, India, Kenya, Malaysia, Hong Kong, Singapore, Siberia, New Zealand, China, Kuwait, the Bahamas, and other fascinating places.

I love to travel, so I always schedule sightseeing days between my workshops. When I presented a workshop in New Delhi for the Creative Communication and Management Center, I gave myself a day to visit the Taj Mahal. While speaking in Russia, I certainly wouldn't miss a visit to Red Square! From there I hopped onto the Trans-Siberian Railway (three nights on the train, you don't want to do that!) to visit Siberia and Mongolia. I always wanted to sleep in a Yurt in the Gobi Desert (you really don't want to do that!).

While teaching at the Hong Kong Management Association and the Malaysian Institute of Management, I managed to cover all of Southeast Asia. One opportunity leads to another and a few years later I went on a speaking tour of the North and South Islands of New Zealand for the New Zealand Association of Executive Secretaries, and then on to tour China, training the managers of the Sheraton Hotels. After my workshop ended, I took off on another dream, crossing the Silk Road of China from Beijing to Kashgar near the Pakistan border. No workshops or keynotes there, the village life hasn't changed in 1000 years. Couldn't resist going to Burma and Cambodia after working in Thailand. Couldn't miss leaving Australia to go to Papua New Guinea, after all it is the most primitive country in the world. No I did not present workshops in the jungles. The natives are still naked and in the stone age!

Seeing and working with other cultures was a great experience for me. If this interests you, let me tell you how to acquire contacts in other parts of the world? What to speak about? And how to handle cultural differences?

WHO DO YOU CONTACT TO SPEAK INTERNATIONALLY?

If you wish to speak internationally, the following information will be helpful.

The United States Chamber of Commerce provides information on American businesses in foreign countries. They have 78 affiliated offices in 70 countries. Their purpose is to develop commercial and economic relations between the United States and the host countries. Also, the World Trade Academy Press will send you lists of major American corporations in most countries that you choose. (See Resources page)

Target the countries you wish to visit, and then target the industry or association in each country that you wish to penetrate. Contact the international headquarters of associations you wish to address. The public library has a reference book of American associations. If you have good information and expertise in an area that they are interested in, they'll be happy to hear from you

The topics of interest are the same as in the United States.

Business management, industry, leadership, communication skills, time management, customer service, Health/wellness, professional development, conflict resolution, empowerment, negotiation, sales skills, team building and all technology fields. BUT all material must be customized to each country. You cannot group all Southeast Asia together as the same culture. There is a vast difference between Hong Kong, Bangkok, Singapore and Malaysia

Many speakers arrange to be presenters on cruise ships. These companies usually offer no monetary compensation, but your cruise is free. However, you may have to pay for your airfare to the departure port and possibly a commission fee to a bureau that specializes in working vacations on cruise ships. (See Resources page)

Consider these other helpful hints:

Arrange multiple engagements in one trip to minimize the overseas air travel time.

Require a signed contract and pre-paid travel expenses. Don't contract to do public seminars with payment based on the number of attendees. I have heard of speakers traveling halfway around the world, only to find that their seminar had been canceled due to poor registration. They received no compensation.

Stipulate that all funds be paid in the form of an International Bank Draft.

Take time to become familiar with the customs and culture of the country you will be visiting. Using the wrong words or gestures can be insulting to your hosts.

If you require a translator, be sure to meet with that person in advance to explain your topic and purpose. If possible, supply your translator with your outline or the text of your presentation. Ask him or her to read it first for interpretation and emphasis. While you're speaking, your eye contact should be with your audience, not the translator. (see Resource page)

Do not use slang expressions or clichés. People in other countries may not understand what "off the wall" or "chill out" means. Use clear and concise language. Speak slowly and use only a few sentences at a time. Be especially careful with humor; it is difficult to translate correctly.

Be aware that icebreakers and interactive audience activities that are used frequently in the United States can be embarrassing for another culture. European and Asian audiences tend to be more formal than U.S. audiences.

Overseas negotiations can be lengthy and very time consuming. Different countries have different concepts of time. In Africa, the Middle East and Asia, the western approach of "time is money" is not as important as building relationships. You must allow time for the "getting to know you" process.

The American negotiation style is informal and quick to adopt a first name basis. Because Europeans and Asians are more formal, address business people by their last name until they request that you address them otherwise. In China, Hong Kong and Singapore, family names come first followed by the given name. Yeo Kwan is referred as Mr. Yeo.

Overseas travel can be exhausting. Allow yourself "jet lag" refueling time — one full day and one full night — before making a presentation.

Always carry the master copy of your speech, workbooks and handouts in your hand luggage. I also always carry one set of business clothes in my hand luggage, just in case my other luggage gets lost. (And it has!)

Carry any medication you think you might need, plus an extra pair of eyeglasses.

As soon as you arrive at your destination, buy a local newspaper. If you are overseas, buy a local paper that is printed in English. This way you can be aware of the happenings and events of your host city.

Recognize that the decision-making process varies from country to country. In Japanese companies, all levels of the corporate hierarchy are carefully consulted before an agreement is reached. German companies prefer to confer only with the department heads. The fastest decision makers are in the United States. In India, all decisions are made by the chief in command. If that person is out of town, nothing gets done.

Speaking of India, their phone system was installed by the British fifty years ago, and only works part of the time. And sometimes street traffic comes to a halt… because the cows are in the street. They have the right of way.

Be aware that power outlets are different in Europe, Asia and Africa. You will need adapters to handle the 220 volts and 50 hertz that you'll find overseas. Most laptops have a switch that changes the currency from 110 to 220. If not, you need to purchase a converter and an adapter.

In Asia, I found that the lunches were more like banquets, and the tea breaks lasted half an hour.

Become familiar with some of the Buddhist, Hindu and Moslem traditions. This way you will understand religious customs, prayer times, and food restrictions.

An excellent source of information for any country is a Culturegram, a four- to six-page summary of culture and customs of the country that interests you. (See Resources page)

Wherever you go, try to allow some time to see the city or countryside. By all means, take a camera with you. Oh, and don't drink the water!

Avoid political commentary on the host country. In fact avoid all political discussion.

Understand and study your host country before you go there. Their pride, history, products. Learn Hello, thank you and goodbye in their language,

When you speak to a diverse audience, whether it is overseas or in the United States, speak a little slower, ask for raised hands if there is anything that needs to be clarified. In this situation allow questions throughout your presentation.

The travel arrangements list and travel checklist on the following pages will make your travel experiences more enjoyable.

SPEAKING ENGAGEMENT
TRAVEL ARRANGEMENTS

Client:

Departure Date: _____ Time: _____
Airline: _____ Flight # _____ Airport:_____
Arrival time: _____ Ground transportation:_____

Contact person:
Phone: _____ Cell phone: _____
Hotel: _____ Address:_____
Phone: _____ Hotel confirmation # _____
Hotel fax # _____

Distance from airport to hotel: _____

Distance from hotel to event: _____

Location & address of event _____
:
Phone # _____ Room _____

Return home date: _____ Time: _____ Airline: _____

Airport: _____ Flight #: _____ Arrival time: _____

Luggage tags _____
Fragile tags for suitcases _____
Colored yarn to easily identify my luggage _____
Frequent Flyer mileage # _____
Hotel awards # _____

TRAVEL CHECKLIST

Tickets
Confirmations
Travelers checks
Photo I.D.
$1 bills for tipping
Credit cards
Envelopes, pens, paper
Paper clips
Rubber bands, stapler
Alarm clock
Travel notebook
Travel iron
Eyeglasses, sunglasses
Contact lens case
Small sewing kit
Rain poncho
Warm sweater
Windbreaker
Scarf, gloves
Hat or sun visor
Camera, film, batteries
Locks for luggage
Butane curling iron
Cosmetics
Walking shoes
Paperback books
Brochures
Business cards
Name tag
Invoice
Envelope for expenses
Script
Master copy of handouts

Master copy of workbooks
Cough drops
Microphone
Tape recorder
Overhead transparencies
35mm slides

INTERNATIONAL

Language dictionary
Passport and passport copies
Visa's and copies
Money conversion chart
Electricity converter
Money belt
Small packets of detergent
Small electric hotpot
Divided envelope for currency
Plastic bags for laundry

"THIRD WORLD" TRAVEL

U.S. Embassy address and phone number
Soap and shampoo
Kleenex
Thermal underwear
Antiseptic soap (Purell)
Swiss army knife
Insect repellant
Decaf coffee packets
Artificial sweetener tablets
Disposable razors
Packages of dried fruit
Small cans of tuna, crackers, trail mix
Gifts: pens, postcards, candy, gum

MEDICATIONS

Antihistamines
Aspirin, Pepto-Bismol
Imodium
Sunscreen
Visine
Small flashlight
Benadryl cream (itch)
Sunburn lotion
Heating pad / ice pack
Eyeglass prescription
Band-Aids
Antibiotics
Cough syrup
Water purification tablets

PERSONAL SPEAKING EVALUATION

Checklist for evaluating your progress:

Did I use confidence-building self-talk techniques to break all barriers?

Did I allow adequate time for preparation?

Was the room arrangement effective and comfortable? Seating?

Temperature? Lighting? Acoustics?

Was my presentation structured? Did I have an attention-grabbing start? Key points? Smooth transitions? A strong close?

Did I use confident gestures? Good eye contact?

Did I use examples, stories, and word pictures?

Did I involve my audience? Did they participate?

How well did I handle questions?

Was I comfortable with props, microphone, audiovisuals?

Did I display enthusiasm?

How did the audience respond to me after the presentation?

What steps should I take to improve?

Students in Malaysia

QUICK REVIEW

QUALITIES OF LEADERSHIP

CONDUCTING MEETINGS

CHECKLISTS FOR MEETINGS

MEETING NOTICE

MEETING ACTION PLAN

CONTROLLING THE MEETING

DIFFICULT PERSONALITIES

MEET THE PRESS

TELEVISION INTERVIEW

CLOTHES & COLORS FOR VIDEO

BECOMING A PAID SPEAKER

SPEAKING CHECKLISTS

A TRAVELING SPEAKER

TRAVEL ARRANGEMENTS

PERSONAL SPEAKING EVALUATION

<u>CLOSING REMARKS</u>

You don't have to be faultless, brilliant and witty, or have perfect diction and a great memory to be a speaker with impact. You do need a strong sense of purpose, respect for your audience — and above all, you have to have a message.

The techniques and tools in this book will boost your self-confidence and strengthen the impact you'll have on your audiences. Every speech that you present will add to your depth of knowledge and experience.

Don't worry about being perfect. Professional speakers often say; "There are three types of speeches: the one you prepare, the one you present, and the one that you wish you had delivered." Your speeches may not be perfect, but most of the time you will be the only one aware of your mistakes or what you forgot to say.

Keep your material current. There is always room for improvement. Continually evaluate yourself, and ask others to evaluate your presentations. Be self-critical but not self-crucifying. Every speaker makes mistakes, so be ready to laugh at yours. Go with the flow, and enjoy the people you meet along the way. Keep in mind that your words can have a lasting effect on people's lives. This power of the platform is awesome.

And now, here's the key, the main ingredient, to successfully presenting every speech, program, and workshop, to relating with every person that you meet — BE ENTHUSIASTIC! Enthusiasm is the zest of life. It brings color, drama and passion to every person you meet.

"Words that come from the heart — enter the heart."
                              —Moses Ibn Ezra

ABOUT THE AUTHOR

Carolyn Kerner Stein is the founder and chief engineer of The Training Express, a corporation that specializes in customer service, leadership and speaking skills. Carolyn has been an international speaker and trainer for over 20 years presenting programs and workshops to major Fortune 500 companies.

Prior to forming her corporation, Carolyn lived in Michigan where she worked on the production of training videos. A gourmet cooking show, many television commercials and feature films.

Carolyn was the founder and first president of the Miami Chapter of the Circumnavigators Club. An International Club of individuals that have circled the globe.

Carolyn is the author of *Passport To The Podium, The Training Express Customer Service Kit, Nifty Networking Tools, The Key To Be, Is Up To Me, The Road Less Traveled Has Ruts And Ridges*

Carolyn and her husband Jerry reside in Florida with their two daughters Linda and Janet, son in law Clifford Stein and five grandsons.

For further information on The Training Express, workshops, coaching, consulting and speaking engagements contact:
Carolyn@carolynstein.com or the trainingexpress.com
www.carolynstein.com

RESOURCES

CONSULTANTS

Jim Barber
The Barber Shop
A coach and business consultant
for speakers
1101 Marcano Blvd.
Plantation, FL 33322-5118
Phone (954)476-9252 Fax (954) 424-0309
Email: jim@thebarbershop.com
www.thebarbershop.com

Dialect Accent Specialists
P.O. Box 44
Lyndonville, VT 05851
(800)753-1016
www.DialectAccentSpecialists.com

Tim Harrises
Graphic Designer
Illustrations, Web design
Phone (954)987-5141
Timharrises@mindspring.com

Candace Hoffmann
Writer and editor
Promotional writing, video production
Phone (561)439-4523
Hoffmannca@aol.com

Donna L. Horkey
Missing Link Consultants, Inc
Human Resource Consulting and Training Services
8211 W. Broward Blvd. Suite PH-1
www.missinglinkconsultants.com
Plantation, FL 33324
Phone (954)577-9700

The Cakov Group
Language Solutions, Inc.
(305)854-8181
www.cakovlanguagesolutions.com
A full service translation and
Interpretation service

Roberta Ruggiero
Founder, President
The Hypoglycemia Support Foundation, Inc.
Information on health and wellness techniques
A one day seminar titled "Are You Healthy Enough For Success"
www.hypoglycemia.org

Terrie Temkin PhD
Non-Profit Management Solutions, Inc
President
Simple Facilitation Tricks to Enliven Any Presentation
http://www.nonprofitmgtsolutions.com/sim_facilitate.html
P.O. Box 7536
Hollywood, FL 33081
(954)985-9489
terriet@nonprofitmanagementsolutions.com
www.nonprofitmanagementsolutions.com

Jeff Zbar
Home Office Organization
Jeff@chiefhomeofficer.com

The Training Express
www.carolynstein.com
carolyn@carolynstein.com
Workshops, coaching, keynotes on
customer service, speaking skills,
leadership, networking
(305)931-3237

ORGANIZATIONS AND ASSOCIATIONS

American Society of Association Executives
1575 I Street NW
Washington D.C 20005
(888)950-2723
www.asaenet.org

American Society of Composers, Authors and Publishers
(ASCAP)
1 Lincoln Plaza
NY, NY 10023
(212) 621-6000

American Society for Training & Development
1640 King Street
Alexandria, VA 22313
Phone (703) 683-8100

Association Central - an extensive searchable directory
Of U.S. based associations plus many international
Associations with contact information
www.associationcentral.com

International Association of Conventions and
Visitors Bureaus
2025 M Street NW
Suite 500
Washington D.C 20036
Phone (202)296-7888

International Special Events Society
401 N. Michigan Ave
Chicago, IL 60611
(312)321-6853

Meeting Professionals International
3030 LBJ Freeway
Suite 1700
Dallas, Texas 75234
(972)702-3000
www.mpiweb.org

The National Speakers Association
1500 S. Priest Drive
Tempe, AZ 85281
Phone (480)968-2552
Fax (480)968-0911
www.nsaspeaker.org

Professional Convention Management Association
Facts and figures regarding the meetings industry
www.pcma.org

Society for Human Resource Management
1800 Duke St
Alexandria, VA 22314-3499
Phone (800)283-SHRM

Toastmasters International
P.O. 9052
Mission Viejo, CA 92690
Phone (949)858-8255
(800) 993-7732
www.toastmasters.org

United States Library of Congress
Washington, D.C.
(202)707-5000

United States Department of Commerce
Washington D.C.
www.commerce.gov

United States Department of Labor
Washington, D.C.
(www.dol.gov

BOOKS AND PERIODICALS FOR RESEARCH & INFORMATION

Ailes, Roger. *You Are The Message.* Doubleday Dell, New York (presentation skills and styles)

Anderson, Peggy. *Great Quotes from Great Leaders.* Career Press, 1997

Beadle, Jeremy. *Today's The Day.* Signet Books, New York (This book lists several events that occur on each day of the year relating to both modern and ancient history.)

Bernstein, Theodore M. *The Reverse Dictionary.* Quadrangle, New York Times Books

Carnegie, Dale. *How to Win Friends and Influence People,* Simon and Schuster, New York

Comedy Writer from Ideascapes
323 Curacao Cove North
Niceville, FL 32576
(904)897-5407

Cooper, Dr. Morton. *Change Your Voice, Change Your Life*
www.voice-doctor.com (310)208-6047

Culturegram
1305 N. Research Way, Bldg. K Orem, UT 84020
Phone (800) 528-6279. Information on foreign customs and cultures

Games Trainers Play, Robert Pike
7620 W 78th St. Edina, MN 55439
Phone (952)829-1954 email: BobPikeCTT@aol.com (ice breakers and team building audience interaction)

Guide to Cruise Ships, Pilot Books
103 Cooper St. Babylon, New York 11702

Helmstetter, Dr. Shad. *What to Say When You Talk to Yourself*
William Morrow, New York. (Exercises in positive self talk)

Kaqne, Joseph Nathan. *Facts about the Presidents.* Ace Books, New York (example: John F. Kennedy was the first president born in the 20th century)

Kane, Joseph Nathan. *Famous First Facts and Records.* Ace Books, New York

Lucaire, Ed. *The Celebrity Book of Lists.* Stein & Day Publishers, New York

Mastering Meetings, 3M Meeting Management Team, McGraw Hill

McKensie, E.C. *14,000 Quips & Quotes for Speakers, Writers, Editors, Preachers and Teachers.* Baker Book House

Motivational Manager. Ragan Communications
316 N. Michigan Ave. #300 Chicago, Illinois 60601   Phone (800) 878-5331   Fax   (312)   960-4140   email: cservice@ragan.com Website:www.ragan.com   (Quotes, statistics and stories for speeches and presentations)

The New York Times (http://www.nytimes.com)

Presentations Magazine covers technology and techniques for creating and designing presentations. www.presentations.com

Resources for Organizations
Training products
(800)383-9210

Speechwriter's Newsletter. Ragan Communications, 316 N. Michigan Ave #300 Chicago, Illinois 60601 Phone (800) 878-5331 Fax (312) 960 4140 Website: www.ragan.com

Successful Meetings Magazine, 355 Park Avenue South, New York 10160 www.successmtgs.com

Uniworld Business Publications, 257 Central Park West Suite 10A New York 10024. Phone (212) 496-2448 (Lists of American companies abroad)

USA Today (http://web.usatoday.com/usafront.htm)

The Wall Street Journal Web site: (http://wsj.com)

Home Office Know-How, Jeffery D. Zbar
P.O. Box 8263 Coral Springs, FL 33075
goingsoho@compuserve.com   www.goingsoho.com

INTERNET INFORMATION AND COMPUTER PROGRAMS

Business Communication
How to communicate more effective on line
In the Internet age
www.espeakonline.com

copy rights
www,copyright.gov

Elance.com
www.elance.com
Web site linking consultants with
potential clients

www.free2fee.com — Free 2 Fee is an online coaching program that guides public speakers to a successful career in professional speaking

www.upyourfee.com — The Up Your Fee Speaker Enrichment Center is the ultimate resource for professional speakers

Harvard Spotlights (Windows) helps you organize, rehearse and deliver presentations.

Inspiration Software, Mind Mapping software, gathers information, outlines and refines the framework of ideas (Mac/Windows)

SMART Technologies, www.smarttech.com (Internet information on conducting meetings)

www.presentersonline.com — Sponsored by Epson tips for creating and designing presentations plus free clip art

www.presentersuniversity.com — This site is sponsored by Proxima, a projector manufacturer and offers presentation tips and techniques

Dynamic Graphics Inc. — www.dgusa.com — subscribe and choose over 5,000 royalty-free images

Medianet. www.medianet-ny.com (seating diagrams)

CrystalGraphics Team, (408) 496-6175   Web: www.powerplugs.com PowerPlugs offer third dimensional transitional effects, charts, and photo effects for PowerPoint

Worlds Greatest Speeches (CD-ROM Windows) Softbit (714)251-9600

Alta Vista - http://www.altavista.digital.com

Excite.netsearch — http://wwwexcite.com

Lycos — http://wwww.lycos.com

Yahoo — http://www.yahoo.com

Census Data - www.census.gov
Internet Public Library - www.ipl.org

Webcasting; www.business.broadcast.com Yahoo Broadcast can deliver end-to-end production services, show direction, rehearsal, moderating and back-end reporting.

Webconferencing; www.placeware.com Meeting Places for small collaborative meetings; Auditorium Places designed for large conferences

Webcasting service provider: E-Conference www.e-conference.com

www.raindance.com Web and phone conferencing on-demand, reservation-less phone conferencing with Web controls

www.webex.com WebEx's services let you share presentations, documents, applications, voice and video spontaneously with anyone, on Windows and Macintosh systems. No setup is required. No uploads and no conversions are needed. The content goes from the presenter's desktop directly to the recipients.

EQUIPMENT

Panasonic Panaboard, 2 Panasonic Way, Secaucus, New Jersey 07094

SMARTBoard, SMART Technologies
Phone (888)42-SMART   Fax (403) 245-0366
Web: www.smarttech.com (an interactive whiteboard with a touch-sensitive surface)

Prompterpeople
(409)353-6000
www.prompterpeople.com

Kodak Digital Projectors
www.kodak.com/go/projectors
(800)242-2424

Delivering Powerful Speeches

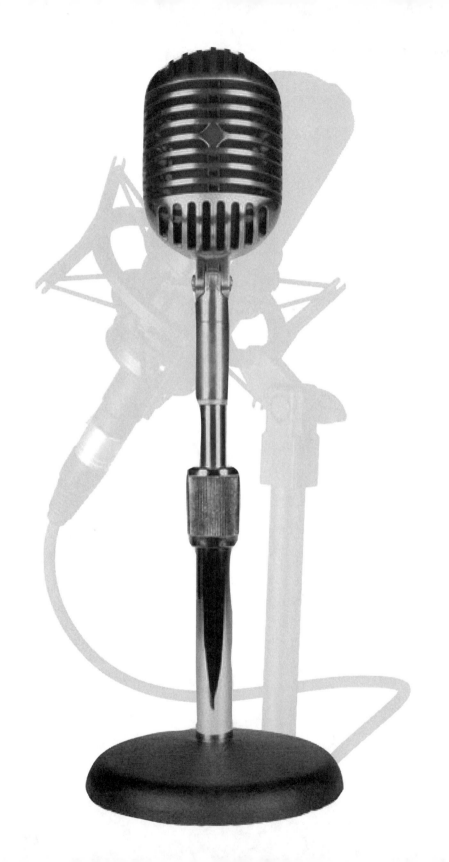

A

Ailes, Roger, 94
Amboseli, Africa, 81
American Society of Association
Executives, 167, 200
American Society of Training and
Development, 148, 167, 200
Analytical Analyzer, 109, 110
Apathetic audience, 125
Audience centered, 15
Audience interaction, 122, 125
Audience involvement, 36, 122
Auditorium, 71

B

Bacall, Lauren, 117
Barber, Jim, 43, 167, 197
Barriers, 3
Beginning your speech, 49
Benny, Jack, 115
Boardroom, 73
Body of your speech, 40
Breakout sessions, 25
Brown, Les, 104
Bush, Barbara, 9, 105
Bush, Laura, 9

Bush, President George, 105
Bush, President George W, 105

C

Carnegie, Dale, 6, 62
Ceremonial speech, 30
Chairing the bored, 149
Challenging Questions, 127
Chambers of Commerce, 166, 174
Chevron, 71
Child, Julia, 117
Churchill, Winston, 104, 106
Classroom style, 71
Clinton, President Bill, 107
Closing remarks, 183
Closing your speech, 47
Clothes and colors, 100, 163
Coaching, 32
Conducting meetings, 143
Consulting, 32
Conversational language, 119
Cooper, Dr. Morton, 120
Creativity, 41
Cronkite, Walter, 104
Cruise ships, 174
Culturegram, 177

D

Dealing with difficult people, 153
Destination management, 168
Digital photography, 88
Document cameras, 88
Dole, Elizabeth, 104
Dole, Robert, 106
Dominant Director, 108, 110
Doors, 75
Drescher, Fran, 117
Dry throat, 17

E

Earn money as a speaker, 164
Electronic whiteboard, 87
Enthusiastic Energetic, 109, 110
Event checklist, 90
Executive briefing, 32
Eyes, 98

F

Fear, 4
Fear solution list, 17
Flipcharts, 85

Fonts, 85
Ford, Betty, 9
Frost, Robert, 113

G

Gestures, 97
Gettysburg Address, 104
Gove, Bill, 63, 107
Graham, Billy, 8
Griffith, Melanie, 117
Group interaction, 122
Guiliani, Rudolph, 141

H

Handout sheets, 56
Harvey, Paul, 104
Hayes, Helen, 9
Hecklers, 133
Helmstetter, Dr. Shad, 14
Henry, Patrick, 49
Home office, 168
Hong Kong Management
 Association, 173
Horkey, Donna, 165, 198
Human Resource Directors, 165

Humor, 44
Hurt, William, 7
Hypoglycemia Support
 Foundation, 198

I

Ice breaker, 125, 126
Impromptu speeches, 29
India, 173
Interact with audience, 122
Introductions, 62

J

Jewelry, 101

K

Keller, Helen, 10
Kennedy, Jacqueline, 117
Kennedy, John F., 104
Kennedy, Robert, 132
Keynote, 22
Keywords, 64

King, Martin Luther, 106

L

Leadership, 140
Lectern, 53, 75
Letter of Agreement, 172
Lighting, 81
Lincoln, Abraham, 21

M

Malaysian Institute, 173
Marcel, Carolyn, 5
Marketing, 164, 168
Mattimore, Bryan, 103
Meeting action plan, 152
Meeting notice, 151
Meeting Professionals, 167
Meeting the press, 156
Meetings, conducting, 143
Meetings checklist, 150
Microphone, 79
Mind mapping, 41
Mispronounced words, 120
Missing Link Consultants, 165
Moderator, 26

Monotone, 117

Moses Ibn Ezra, 183

Mother Theresa, 107, 156

Motivational speeches, 25

Mumblers, 118

Music, 83

Music stand, 52

N

National Speakers Assoc., 63, 167

Nervous gestures, 96

Networking, 169

New technology for meet-
ings,87,145

New Zealand, 173

Nixon, Richard, 107

NonProfit Management, 146

Non-verbal, 94

Noonan, Peggie, 106

Notes, 51

O

Ophrah Winfrey, 104

Osmond, Donny, 7

Outline of speech structure, 40

Overhead projector, 85

Overhead transparencies, 85

Overseas negotiation, 175

P

Panaboard, 87

Panel discussion, 26

Pause, 114

Peale, Dr. Norman Vincent, 7

Pitfalls, 133-136

Pointing, 97

Political speech, 31

Porter, Cole, 69

Posture, 95

Powell, General Colin, 107

PowerPoint, 87

Preparing your speech, 35

Press kit, 159, 168

Professional speaking, 164

Projection screen, 75

Proxima, 87

Public speaking, 22

Publicity, 164

Q

Questions, 127
Questions, hostile, 130
Questions, difficult, 128

R

Reagan, Ronald, 50, 105
Rehearse, 58
Reliable Responsive, 109, 110
Republican National Convention, 8
Research, 38
Resources, 197
Risk, 11
Robbins, Tony, 25, 104
Roberts Rules, 147
Room arrangements, 70, 72
Room chairman, 70
Rooney, Andy, 45, 62
Roosevelt, Franklin D., 104
Rotary, 166
Round tables, 71
Ruggiero, Roberta, 198
Russia, 173

S

Sales, 24

Sales presentation, 24
Sandberg, Carl, 106
Sanford markers, 84
Schwarzkopf, General Norman, 104
Self promotion, 156
Self talk, 13
Selleck, Tom, 8
Siberia, 173
Sorensen, Ted, 104
Southeast Asia, 173
Speakers Bureaus, 168
Speakers evaluation form, 184
Speaking engagement travel list, 178
Speaking, event checklist, 171
Speaking, with style, 103
Special event planners, 168
Seminar, 23
Stallone, Sly, 117
Stage fright, 7
Stories, 44
Streisand, Barbra, 7
Structure of your speech, 40
Style, 103
Style, defining yours, 108
Symbols, 52
T

Teachno-speak, 119

Technical presentation, 27

Technostress, 119

Teleprompter, 78

Television checklist, 162

Temkin, Terrie, 146, 198

Temperature, room, 78

Theater style, 71

Thurber, James, 46

Titles, 50

Toastmasters International,13, 167

Topic, 35

Training, 32

Training Express, 166

Trans Siberian, 173

Translator, 175

Transparencies, 85

Travel checklist, 179

Traveling speaker, 173

Truman, Harry, 106

Turner, Kathleen, 117

Twain, Mark, 31

V

Video checklist, 162

Video conferencing, 146

Video, making an appearance, 161

Visitors and Convention Bureau, 168

Visual aids, 84

W

Wall Street Journal, 145

Web- conferencing, 89, 146

Web-casting, 89, 146

Weldon, Joel, 38

West, Mae, 108

Word power, 113

Workbooks, 56

Worksheets, 56

World Wide Web, 89

World Trade Academy Press, 174

U

U shaped tables, 71, 73

U.S. Chamber of Commerce, 174

Up Your Fee 6, 167

Z

Zbar, Jeffrey, 168, 199

Zig Zigler, 25, 89, 104

Zukov, 5